WIGWAM EVENINGS

THE STRANGER WATCHES THE LAUGH-MAKER AND THE BEARS.

[FRONTISPIECE. *See page* 189

WIGWAM EVENINGS

SIOUX FOLK TALES RETOLD

BY CHARLES A. EASTMAN
(*Ohiyesa*)

AND ELAINE GOODALE EASTMAN

Illustrated by Edwin Willard Deming

Introduction by Michael Dorris and
Louise Erdrich

University of Nebraska Press
Lincoln and London

Introduction copyright © 1990 by the University of
Nebraska Press
Manufactured in the United States of America

First Bison Book printing: 1990
Most recent printing indicated by the last digit below:
10   9   8   7   6   5   4   3   2   1

Library of Congress Cataloging-in-Publication Data
Eastman, Charles Alexander, 1858–1939.
Wigwam evenings: Sioux folk tales retold / by Charles A. Eastman and Elaine Goodale Eastman: introduction by Michael Dorris and Louise Erdrich.
p.   cm.
Reprint. Originally published: Boston: Little, Brown, 1909.
"A Bison Book."
ISBN 0-8032-1815-X
ISBN 0-8032-6717-7 (pbk.)
1. Dakota Indians—Legends. I. Eastman, Elaine Goodale, 1863–
1953. II. Title.
E99.D1E183   1990
398.2′089975—dc20
90-35728 CIP

Originally published in 1909 by Little, Brown and Company. The
preface has been dropped from this Bison Book edition.

NOTE

*The authors wish to acknowledge the courtesy of the Ladies'
Home Journal, Good Housekeeping, and the Woman's Home
Companion, in giving permission to include in this volume several
stories which first appeared in their pages.*

∞

CONTENTS

ILLUSTRATIONS

INTRODUCTION
by Michael Dorris and Louise Erdrich

Fables cross cultural boundaries with particular ease because they are often stories that tap into primal human emotions, fears and hopes. They are not so much specifically intended for the moral education of children as they are required to be accessible to listeners of all ages, resonating with different shades of meaning depending on whether the audience is very young, adult, or elderly. Furthermore, as a key part of a people's oral tradition, fables must be sufficiently entertaining to allow frequent retellings without boredom, and they must be memorable enough to be passed on almost verbatim.

Smoky Day—the wise sage who relates the nightly episodes of *Wigwam Evenings* to, among others, an enraptured boy and girl named Wasula and Chatanna—prefaces his twenty-sixth installment with, "I hope that you have listened so well to these tales of our people, and repeated them so often that you will never forget them." He continues, "We must not only remember and repeat . . . but we must consider and follow their teachings, for it is so that these legends that have come down to us from the old time are kept alive by each new generation."

Aesop knew this when he recorded for the first time the simple Greek maxims, couched in quixotic, anthropomorphic animal adventures. The Uncle Remus cycles are based on the same sort of pedagogical shorthand: don't do this, the stories communicate, because look what happened to the hare (or to Br'er Rabbit) when he tried the same thing! "It is not a wise thing to boast too loudly," goes the moral of Smoky Day's "Second Evening." Other vignettes are equally direct: Don't be smug, improvident, gullible, immodest, greedy. Don't trust strangers too readily. Keep your promises. Work hard, do your best, have hope, be resourceful.

The foundations for Sioux cosmology, polity, and social intercourse can be discovered in the body of *Wigwam Evenings*. Physician, scholar, author Charles Eastman (Ohiyesa), in collaboration with his wife, Elaine Goodale Eastman, has assembled in this collection a composite, condensed sampling of his tribe's values, and presents them in a language that is at once direct and engaging. To say these allegories are "wise" begs the question; they are the distilled conclusions of generations upon generations of Plains society and point to the essence of what it is to be a decent, thoughtful, respectable human being—a Sioux *Tao* told in prose a child of any culture, of any time, can comprehend.

"Observe," the legend-teller points out on the first evening, "that silence is greater than speech. This is why we honor the animals, who are more silent than man, and we reverence the trees and rocks, where the Great Mystery lives undisturbed, in a peace that is never broken."

Sprinkled throughout *Wigwam Evenings* are the seeds of Sioux thought, legends of monsters, origin myths accounting for the presence in the world of war and strife. But as the accumulation of stories progresses, three-dimensional characters are increasingly introduced. Halfway through the book we meet the Little Boy Man, whom Eastman in his introduction calls the "Adam" of the Sioux. Unlike mankind's progenitor from "Genesis," however, this first man turns out to have been far from an intentional creation—instead, he derived from a splinter in the Great Spirit's big toe! And his chief adversary is not some core of internal weakness, some inherent temptation toward disobedience, but rather the very obvious danger of hostile nature and wild animals, who resent his intrusion into *their* Garden.

The Little Boy Man is our precedent-setter, our direct example of both human foible and strength. We identify with his confusions, sympathize with his mistakes, rejoice at his triumphs. He is a clear link between the wholly imaginary and real life, and as such is a stand-in for a child struggling to learn the rules that govern day-to-day existence.

Certainly no mere month of listenings after sundown can convey the finer complexities of traditional Sioux life, but this round of stories does establish a context in which those underlying concepts may be fruitfully examined. "There are wonders all about us, and within," Smoky Day observes on the last (twenty-seventh) evening, "but if we are quiet and obedient to the voice of the spirit, sometime we may understand these mysteries!"

By describing the ideal, by defining the outer limits of acceptable social behaviors and the consequences of their violation, *Wigwam Evenings* affords a fantastical and intellectual penetration of a society at once drastically unfamiliar to contemporary non-Sioux readers and instantly recognizable at its core as practical, common-sense experience. And no matter how blurred the boundary between past and present, between the realms of beastly and of human dominance, between unpredictable ghosts and pragmatic logic, this rich collection from another time and place offers a contemporary message of great ultimate solace: "There is no magic so strong that it will prevail against true love."

Michael Dorris is the author of *A Yellow Raft in Blue Water* (1987), *Native Americans: Five Hundred Years After* (1975), and *The Broken Cord* (1989). Louise Erdrich is the author of two volumes of poetry and three novels, *Love Medicine* (1984), *The Beet Queen* (1986), and *Tracks* (1988). Married since 1981, they often collaborate in their work.

FIRST EVENING

THE BUFFALO AND THE FIELD-MOUSE

WIGWAM EVENINGS

FIRST EVENING

THE cold December moon is just showing above the tree-tops, pointing a white finger here and there at the clustered teepees of the Sioux, while opposite their winter camp on the lake shore a lonely, wooded island is spread like a black buffalo robe between the white, snow-covered ice and the dull gray sky.

All by itself at the further end of the village stands the teepee of Smoky Day, the old story-teller, the school-master of the woods. The paths that lead to this low brown wigwam are well beaten;

deep, narrow trails, like sheep paths, in the hard-frozen snow.

To-night a generous fire of logs gives both warmth and light inside the teepee, and the˘old man is calmly filling his long, red pipe for the smoke of meditation, when the voices and foot-steps of several children are distinctly heard through the stillness of the winter night.

The door-flap is raised, and the nine-year-old Tanagela, the Humming-bird, slips in first, with her roguish black eyes and her shy smile.

" Grandmother, we have come to hear a story," she murmurs. " I have brought you a sun-dried buffalo-tongue, grand-mother! "

One by one the little people of the village follow her, and all seat them-selves on the ground about the central fire until the circle is well filled. Then the old man lays down his pipe, clears

SMOKY DAY TELLING TALES OF OLD DAYS AROUND HIS FIRE.

his throat once or twice and begins in a serious voice:

" These old stories for which you ask teach us the way of life, my grand-children. The Great-Grandfather of all made us all; therefore we are brothers.

" In many of the stories the people have a common language, which now the Great Mystery has taken away from us, and has put a barrier between us and them, so that we can no longer converse together and understand the speech of the animal people.

" Observe, further, that silence is greater than speech. This is why we honor the animals, who are more silent than man, and we reverence the trees and rocks, where the Great Mystery lives undisturbed, in a peace that is never broken.

" Let no one ask a question until the story is finished."

THE BUFFALO AND THE FIELD-MOUSE

Once upon a time, when the Field-Mouse was out gathering wild beans for the winter, his neighbor, the Buffalo, came down to graze in the meadow. This the little Mouse did not like, for he knew that the other would mow down all the long grass with his prickly tongue, and there would be no place in which to hide. He made up his mind to offer battle like a man.

" Ho, Friend Buffalo, I challenge you to a fight! " he exclaimed in a small, squeaking voice.

The Buffalo paid no attention, no doubt thinking it only a joke. The Mouse angrily repeated the challenge, and still his enemy went on quietly grazing. Then the little Mouse laughed with contempt as he offered his defiance. The Buffalo at last looked at him and replied carelessly:

" You had better keep still, little one, or I shall come over there and step on you, and there will be nothing left! "

" You can't do it! " replied the Mouse.

" I tell you to keep still," insisted the Buffalo, who was getting angry. " If you speak to me again, I shall certainly come and put an end to you! "

" I dare you to do it! " said the Mouse, provoking him.

Thereupon the other rushed upon him. He trampled the grass clumsily and tore up the earth with his front hoofs. When he had ended, he looked for the Mouse, but he could not see him anywhere.

" I told you I would step on you, and there would be nothing left! " he muttered.

Just then he felt a scratching inside his right ear. He shook his head as hard as he could, and twitched his ears back and forth. The gnawing went deeper and deeper until he was half wild with the pain. He pawed with his hoofs and tore up the sod with his horns. Bellowing madly, he ran as fast as he could, first straight forward and then in circles, but at last he stopped and stood trembling. Then the Mouse jumped out of his ear, and said:

"Will you own now that I am master?"

"No!" bellowed the Buffalo, and again he started toward the Mouse, as if to trample him under his feet. The little fellow was nowhere to be seen, but in a minute the Buffalo felt him in the other ear. Once more he became wild with pain, and ran here and there over the prairie, at times leaping high in the air. At last he fell to the ground and lay quite still. The Mouse came out of his ear, and stood proudly upon his dead body.

" Eho! " said he, " I have killed the greatest of all beasts. This will show to all that I am master! "

Standing upon the body of the dead Buffalo, he called loudly for a knife with which to dress his game.

In another part of the meadow, Red Fox, very hungry, was hunting mice for his breakfast. He saw one and jumped upon him with all four feet, but the little Mouse got away, and he was dreadfully disappointed.

All at once he thought he heard a distant call: " Bring a knife! Bring a knife! "

When the second call came, Red Fox started in the direction of the sound. At the first knoll he stopped and listened, but hearing nothing more, he was about to go back. Just then he heard the call plainly, but in a very thin voice, " Bring a knife! " Red Fox immediately set out again and ran as fast as he could.

By and by he came upon the huge body of the Buffalo lying upon the ground. The little Mouse still stood upon the body.

"I want you to dress this Buffalo for me and I will give you some of the meat," commanded the Mouse.

"Thank you, my friend, I shall be glad to do this for you," he replied, politely.

The Fox dressed the Buffalo, while the Mouse sat upon a mound near by, looking on and giving his orders. "You must cut the meat into small pieces," he said to the Fox. When the Fox had finished his work, the Mouse paid him with a small piece of liver. He swallowed it quickly and smacked his lips.

"Please, may I have another piece?" he asked quite humbly.

"Why, I gave you a very large piece!
How greedy you are!" exclaimed the
Mouse. "You may have some of the
blood clots," he sneered. So the poor
Fox took the blood clots and even licked
off the grass. He was really very hungry.

"Please may I take home a piece of
the meat?" he begged. "I have six
little folks at home, and there is nothing
for them to eat."

"You can take the four feet of the
Buffalo. That ought to be enough for
all of you!"

"Hi, hi! Thank you, thank you!"
said the Fox. "But, Mouse, I have a
wife also, and we have had bad luck
in hunting. We are almost starved.
Can't you spare me a little more?"

"Why," declared the Mouse, "I have
already overpaid you for the little work
you have done. However, you can take
the head, too!"

Thereupon the Fox jumped upon the Mouse, who gave one faint squeak and disappeared.

If you are proud and selfish you will lose all in the end.

SECOND EVENING
THE FROGS AND THE CRANE

SECOND EVENING

AGAIN the story-hour is come, and the good old wife of the legend-teller has made her poor home as warm and pleasant as may be, in expectation of their guests. She is proud of her husband's honorable position as the village teacher, and makes all the children welcome, as they arrive, with her shrill-voiced, cheerful greeting:

"Han, han; sit down, sit down; that is right, that is very right, my grandchild!"

To-night the Humming-bird has come leading by the hand her small brother, who stumbles along in his fringed, leathern leggings and handsomely beaded moccasins, his chubby, solemn face fin-

ished off with two long, black braids
tied with strips of otter-skin.   As he is
inclined to be restless and to talk out
of season, she keeps him close beside her.

" It is cold to-night! " he pipes up
suddenly when all is quiet.   " Why do
we not listen to these stories in the warm
summer-time, elder sister? "

" Hush, my little brother! " Tanagela
reproves him with a frightened look.
" Have you never heard that if the old
stories are told in summer, the snakes
will creep into our beds? " she whispers
fearfully.

" That is true, my granddaughter,"
assents the old man.   " Yet we may tell
a legend of summer days to comfort
the heart of the small brother! "

THE FROGS AND THE CRANE

In the heart of the woods there lay a
cool, green pond.   The shores of the

pond were set with ranks of tall bul-
rushes that waved crisply in the wind,
and in the shallow bays there were fleets
of broad water lily leaves. Among the
rushes and reeds and in the quiet water
there dwelt a large tribe of Frogs.

On every warm night of spring, the
voices of the Frogs arose in a cheerful
chorus. Some voices were low and deep
— these were the oldest and wisest of
the Frogs; at least, they were old enough
to have learned wisdom. Some were
high and shrill, and these were the voices
of the little Frogs who did not like to
be reminded of the days when they
had tails and no legs.

"Kerrump! kerrump! I'm chief of this
pond!" croaked a very large bullfrog,
sitting in the shade of a water lily leaf.

"Kerrump! kerrump! I'm chief of
this pond!" replied a hoarse voice from
the opposite bank.

" Kerrump! kerrump! I'm chief of this pond!" boasted a third old Frog from the furthest shore of the pond.

Now a long-legged white Crane was standing near by, well hidden by the coarse grass that grew at the water's edge. He was very hungry that evening, and when he heard the deep voice of the first Bullfrog he stepped briskly up to him and made a quick pass under the broad leaf with his long, cruel bill. The old Frog gave a frightened croak, and kicked violently in his efforts to get away, while over the quiet pond, splash! splash! went the startled little Frogs into deep water.

The Crane almost had him, when something cold and slimy wound itself about one of his legs. He drew back for a second, and the Frog got safely away! But the Crane did not lose his dinner after all, for about his leg was curled

a large black water snake, and that made
a fair meal.

Now he rested awhile on one leg, and
listened. The first Frog was silent, but
from the opposite bank the second Frog
croaked boastfully:

" Kerrump! kerrump! I'm chief of
this pond!"

The Crane began to be hungry again.
He went round the pond without making
any noise, and pounced upon the second
Frog, who was sitting up in plain sight,
swelling his chest with pride, for he
really thought now that he was the sole
chief of the pond.

The Crane's head and most of his long
neck disappeared under the water, and
all over the pond the little Frogs went
splash! splash! into the deepest holes
to be out of the way.

Just as he had the Frog by one hind
leg, the Crane saw something that made

him let go, flap his broad wings and fly awkwardly away to the furthest shore. It was a mink, with his slender brown body and wicked eyes, and he had crept very close to the Crane, hoping to seize him at his meal! So the second Frog got away too; but he was so dreadfully frightened that he never spoke again.

After a long time the Crane got over his fright and he became very hungry once more. The pond had been still so long that many of the Frogs were singing their pleasant chorus, and above them all there boomed the deep voice of the third and last Bullfrog, saying:

"Kerrump! kerrump! I'm chief of this pond!"

The Crane stood not far from the boaster, and he determined to silence him once for all. The next time he began to speak, he had barely said "Kerrump!" when the Crane had him by the

leg. He croaked and struggled in vain,
and in another moment he would have
gone down the Crane's long throat.

But just then a Fox crept up behind

the Crane and seized *him!* The Crane
let go the Frog and was carried off
screaming into the woods for the Fox's
supper. So the third Frog got away;

but he was badly lamed by the Crane's strong bill, and he never dared to open his mouth again.

It is not a wise thing to boast too loudly.

THIRD EVENING
THE EAGLE AND THE BEAVER

THIRD EVENING

"NO, elder sister, it is not for a hunter and a brave to fetch wood for the lodge fire! That is woman's task, and it is not right that you should ask it of me."

"But see, my younger brother, you are only a small boy and can neither hunt nor fight; surely, therefore, it is well for you to help our mother at home!"

The two children, Wasula and Chatanna, as they draw near the old storyteller's wigwam, are carrying on a dispute that has arisen between them earlier in the evening, when dry sticks were to be gathered for cooking the supper, and Chatanna, aged seven, refused to help his sister on the ground that it is not a warrior's duty to provide wood. Both appeal to their teacher to settle the question.

" Hun, hun, hay! " good-naturedly exclaims the old man. " Truly, there is much to be said on both sides; but perhaps you can agree more easily after you have heard my story."

THE EAGLE AND THE BEAVER

Out of the quiet blue sky there shot like an arrow the great War-eagle. Beside the clear brown stream an old Beaver - woman was busily chopping wood. Yet she was not too busy to catch the whir of descending wings, and the Eagle reached too late the spot where she had vanished in the midst of the shining pool.

He perched sullenly upon a dead tree

near by and kept his eyes steadily upon the smooth sheet of water above the dam.

After a time the water was gently stirred and a sleek, brown head cautiously appeared above it.

" What right have you," reproached the Beaver-woman, " to disturb thus the mother of a peaceful and hard-working people? "

" Ugh, I am hungry," the Eagle replied shortly.

" Then why not do as we do — let other folks alone and work for a living? "

" That is all very well for you," the Eagle retorted, " but not everybody can cut down trees with his teeth, or live upon bark and weeds in a mud-plastered wigwam. I am a warrior, not an old woman! "

" It is true that some people are born trouble-makers," returned the Beaver, quietly. "Yet I see no good reason why you, as well as we, should not be content with plain fare and willing to toil for what you want. My work, moreover, is of use to others besides myself and family, for with my dam-building I deepen the stream for the use of all the dwellers therein, while you are a terror to all living creatures that are weaker than yourself. You would do well to profit by my example."

So saying, she dove down again to the bottom of the pool.

The Eagle waited patiently for a long time, but he saw nothing more of her; and so, in spite of his contempt for the harm-less industry of an old Beaver-woman, it was he, not she, who was obliged to go hungry that morning.

Pride alone will not fill the stomach.

FOURTH EVENING

THE WAR-PARTY

FOURTH EVENING

THERE is no greater rudeness than to interrupt a story-teller, even by the slightest movement. All Sioux children are drilled in this rule of behavior, as in many others, from their earliest babyhood, and old Smoky Day has seldom to complain of any lack of attention. Even Teona and Waola, active boys of eleven and twelve, and already daring hunters, would be ashamed to draw upon themselves by word or motion the reproving looks of their mates. A disturbance so serious as to deserve the notice of the old teacher himself would disgrace them all!

" Although we shall hear again of the animal people," he begins pleasantly but with due gravity, " and even of some who are not animals at all, we must remember that each of these warriors of whom I shall tell you really represents a man, and the special weakness of each should remind us to inquire of our own weakness. In this life, it is often the slow one who wins in the end; and this we shall now see!"

THE WAR - PARTY

One day the Turtle made ready to go upon the war-path. His comrades who wished to go with him were Live Coals, Ashes, the Bulrush, the Grasshopper, the Dragonfly and the Pickerel. All seven warriors went on in good spirits to the first camp, where a strong wind arose in the early morning and blew the Ashes away.

" Iho!" exclaimed the others, " this one was no warrior!"

The six kept on their way, and the second day they came to a river. There Live Coals perished at the crossing. "S-s-s," he said, and was gone!

"Ah!" declared the five, "it is easy to see that he could not fight!"

On the further side of the river they looked back, and saw that the Bulrush had stayed behind. He stood still and waved his hand to the others, who grumbled among themselves, saying:

"He was no true brave, that one!"

The four who were left went on till they came to a swampy place, and there the Grasshopper stuck fast. In his struggles to get out of the bog he pulled both legs off, and so there were only three to go upon the war-path!

The Dragonfly mourned for his friend. He cried bitterly, and finally blew his nose so hard that his slender neck broke in two.

" Ah! " declared the other two, " we are better off without those feeble ones! "

The Pickerel and the Turtle, being left alone, advanced bravely into the country of the enemy. At the head of the lake they were met and quickly surrounded. The Pickerel escaped by swimming, but the Turtle, that slow one, was caught!

They took him to the village, and there the head men held a council to decide what should be done with him.

" We will build a fire and roast him alive in the midst of it," one proposed.

" Hi-i-i! " the Turtle shrilled his war-cry. " That is the brave death I would choose! I shall trample the fire, and scatter live coals among the people! "

" No," declared another, " we will boil water and throw him into the pot! "

" Hi-i-i! " again cried the Turtle. " I shall dance in the boiling pot, and clouds of steam will arise to blind the eyes of the people!"

The counsellors looked doubtfully at one another, and at last one said:

"Why not carry him out to the middle of the lake and drown him?"

Then the Turtle drew in his head and became silent.

"Alas!" he groaned, "that is the only death I fear!"

So the people took him in a canoe, and rowed out to the middle of the lake. There they dropped him in, and he sank like a stone!

But the next minute he came up to the top of the water and again uttered his war-cry.

"Hi-i-i!" he cried. "Now I am at home!" And he dived and swam wherever he would.

This story teaches us that *patience and quick wit are better than speed.*

FIFTH EVENING
THE FALCON AND THE DUCK

FIFTH EVENING

THE boaster is a well-known character in every Indian village;
and it is quite plain from the
number of stories warning us against
self-praise, that the wise men of the tribe
have not been slow to discover and point
out this weakness of their people.

The stories told by Smoky Day are
seldom without a moral, and we may
be sure that the children are not sent
to him only to be entertained, but also
to learn and profit by the stored-up
wisdom of the past. Moreover, they are
expected afterward to repeat the tales
in the family circle, and there is much
rivalry among the little folks as to who
shall tell them best. Teona has a good

memory and ready wit, and his versions are commonly received with approval, but it happens that little Tanagela, his cousin, has just won a triumph by her sprightly way of telling the fourth evening's tale of the seven warriors. The little maid listens to-night with burning cheeks and shining eyes, eager to repeat her success with the pretty story of

THE FALCON AND THE DUCK

The wintry winds had already begun to whistle and the waves to rise when the Drake and his mate gathered their half-grown brood together on the shores of their far northern lake.

" Wife," said he, " it is now time to take the children southward, to the Warm Countries which they have never yet seen! "

Very early the next morning they set out on their long journey, forming

a great V against the sky in their flight.
The mother led her flock and the father
brought up the rear, keeping a sharp
lookout for stragglers.

All day they flew high in the keen
air, over wide prairies and great forests of
northern pine, until toward evening they
saw below them a chain of lakes, glit-
tering like a string of dark-blue stones.

Swinging round in a half circle, they dropped lower and lower, ready to alight and rest upon the smooth surface of the nearest lake.

Suddenly their leader heard a whizzing sound like that of a bullet as it cuts the air, and she quickly gave the warning: " Honk! honk! Danger, danger!" All descended in dizzy spirals, but as the great Falcon swooped toward them with upraised wing, the ducklings scattered wildly hither and thither. The old Drake came last, and it was he who was struck!

" Honk, honk!" cried all the Ducks in terror, and for a minute the air was full of soft downy feathers like flakes of snow. But the force of the blow was lost upon the well-cushioned body of the Drake, he soon got over his fright and went on his way southward with his family, while the Falcon dropped heavily to the water's edge with a broken wing.

There he stayed and hunted mice as best he could from day to day, sleeping at night in a hollow log to be out of the way of the Fox and the Weasel. All the wit he had was not too much whereby to keep himself alive through the long, hard winter.

Toward spring, however, the Falcon's wing had healed and he could fly a little, though feebly. The sun rose higher and higher in the blue heavens, and the Ducks began to return to their cool northern home. Every day a flock or two flew over the lake; but the Falcon dared not charge upon the flocks, much as he wished to do so. He was weak with hunger, and afraid to trust to the strength of the broken wing.

One fine day a chattering flock of Mallards alighted quite near him, cooling their glossy breasts upon the gently rippling wave.

" Here, children," boasted an old Drake, " is the very spot where your father was charged upon last autumn by a cruel Falcon! I can tell you that it took all my skill and quickness in dodging to save my life. Best of all, our fierce enemy dropped to the ground with a broken wing! Doubtless he is long since dead of starvation, or else a Fox or a Mink has made a meal of the wicked creature! "

By these words the Falcon knew his old enemy, and his courage returned.

" Nevertheless, I am still here! " he exclaimed, and darted like a flash upon the unsuspecting old Drake, who was resting and telling of his exploit and narrow escape with the greatest pride and satisfaction.

" Honk! honk! " screamed all the

Ducks, and they scattered and whirled upward like the dead leaves in autumn; but the Falcon with sure aim selected the old Drake and gave swift chase. Round and round in dizzy spirals they swung together, till with a quick spurt the Falcon struck the shining, outstretched neck of the other, and snapped it with one powerful blow of his reunited wing.

Do not exult too soon; nor is it wise to tell of your brave deeds within the hearing of your enemy.

SIXTH EVENING

THE RACCOON AND THE BEE-TREE

SIXTH EVENING

"HO, Chatanna," says the old story-teller, pleasantly, " I see that you have brought Mato, the Bear, with you to-night! I hope he will be good and not disturb the other scholars."

" Grandfather," says Chatanna, earnestly, " he will be good. He obeys me, and is never troublesome like some pets. He will lie quietly here by me and listen to the story!"

All the children range themselves around the brightly burning fire, the little boys sitting cross-legged, and the girls sideways, like demure little women.

Although they do not know it yet, there is a special treat in store for them all this evening. The story is one in which feasting plays a part, and whenever good things to eat come into a story, it is a pleasant custom of the Sioux to offer some delicacy.

The good old wife of the teacher has prepared a kettle full of her choicest wild rice, dark in color but of a flavor to be remembered, and a generous dish of boiled rice sprinkled with maple-sugar is passed to each child, (and doubtless shared with Mato by his loving friend,) at the close of the story about

THE RACCOON AND THE BEE - TREE

The Raccoon had been asleep all day in the snug hollow of a tree. The dusk was coming on when he awoke, stretched himself once or twice, and jumping down from the top of the tall, dead stump in which he made his home, set out to look for his supper.

In the midst of the woods there was a lake, and all along the lake shore there rang out the alarm cries of the water people as the Raccoon came nearer and nearer.

First the Swan gave a scream of warning. The Crane repeated the cry, and from the very middle of the lake the Loon, swimming low, took it up and echoed it back over the still water.

The Raccoon sped merrily on, and finding no unwary bird that he could seize he picked up a few mussel-shells from the beach, cracked them neatly and ate the sweet meat.

A little further on, as he was leaping hither and thither through the long, tangled meadow grass, he landed with all four feet on a family of Skunks — father, mother and twelve little ones, who were curled up sound asleep in a soft bed of broken dry grass.

" Huh!" exclaimed the father Skunk.
" What do you mean by this, eh?"
And he stood looking at him defiantly.

" Oh, excuse me, excuse me," begged

the Raccoon. " I am very sorry. I did
not mean to do it! I was just running
along and I did not see you at all."

" Better be careful where you step next
time," grumbled the Skunk, and the
Raccoon was glad to hurry on.

Running up a tall tree he came upon two red Squirrels in one nest, but before he could get his paws upon one of them they were scolding angrily from the topmost bough.

"Come down, friends!" called the Raccoon. "What are you doing up there? Why, I wouldn't harm you for anything!"

"Ugh, you can't fool us," chattered the Squirrels, and the Raccoon went on.

Deep in the woods, at last, he found a great hollow tree which attracted him by a peculiar sweet smell. He sniffed and sniffed, and went round and round till he saw something trickling down a narrow crevice. He tasted it and it was deliciously sweet.

He ran up the tree and down again, and at last found an opening into which he could thrust his paw. He brought it out covered with honey!

Now the Raccoon was happy. He ate and scooped, and scooped and ate the golden, trickling honey with both forepaws till his pretty, pointed face was daubed all over.

Suddenly he tried to get a paw into his ear. Something hurt him terribly just then, and the next minute his sensitive nose was frightfully stung. He rubbed his face with both sticky paws. The sharp stings came thicker and faster, and he wildly clawed the air. At last he forgot to hold on to the branch any longer, and with a screech he tumbled to the ground.

There he rolled and rolled on the dead leaves till he was covered with leaves from head to foot, for they stuck to his fine, sticky fur, and most of all they covered his eyes and his striped face. Mad with fright and pain he dashed through

SO THEY RAN AND THEY RAN OUT OF THE WOODS ON TO THE
SHINING WHITE BEACH.

the forest calling to some one of his own
kind to come to his aid.

The moon was now bright, and many
of the woods people were abroad. A
second Raccoon heard the call and went
to meet it. But when he saw a frightful
object plastered with dry leaves racing
madly toward him he turned and ran
for his life, for he did not know what
this thing might be.

The Raccoon who had been stealing
the honey ran after him as fast as he
could, hoping to overtake and beg the
other to help him get rid of his leaves.

So they ran and they ran out of the
woods on to the shining white beach
around the lake. Here a Fox met them,
but after one look at the queer object
which was chasing the frightened Raccoon he too turned and ran at his best
speed.

Presently a young Bear came loping out

of the wood and sat up on his haunches to see them go by. But when he got a good look at the Raccoon who was plastered with dead leaves, he scrambled up a tree to be out of the way.

By this time the poor Raccoon was so frantic that he scarcely knew what he was doing. He ran up the tree after the Bear and got hold of his tail.

" Woo, woo! " snarled the Bear, and the Raccoon let go. He was tired out and dreadfully ashamed. He did now what he ought to have done at the very first — he jumped into the lake and washed off most of the leaves. Then he got back to his hollow tree and curled himself up and licked and licked his soft fur till he had licked himself clean, and then he went to sleep.

The midnight hunter steals at his own risk.

SEVENTH EVENING

THE BADGER AND THE BEAR

SEVENTH EVENING

THE night is cold and clear, with a full moon overhead, and soon after supper Tanagela appears in her snug doeskin gown and warm robe of the same, tanned with the hair on, drawing her little brother in a great turtle-shell over the crusty snow.

Old Smoky Day laughs heartily at the sight, standing just outside his teepee door to watch for the coming of the children. Nor is this all, for in the wake of this pair comes another dragging a rude sled made of a buffalo's ribs, well covered with soft furs, while still another has borrowed his mother's large raw-hide for the occasion. After their frolicsome ride through the brightly lighted village, they are all in a happy mood, ready to listen to the interesting story of

THE BADGER AND THE BEAR

The Badger lived in a little house under the hill and it was warm and snug. Here, too, lived mother Badger and the little Badgers, and they were fat and merry, for the gray old Badger was a famous hunter. Folks said he must have a magic art in making arrows, since he never failed to bring in meat enough and to spare!

One day, father Badger stayed at home to make new arrows. His wife was busy slicing and drying the meat left over from the hunt of the day before, while the little ones played at hide-and-go-seek about the lodge.

All at once, a big, clumsy shape darkened the low doorway. The children hid their faces in fear, but father Badger got up and welcomed the stranger kindly. He was a large black Bear. His shaggy skin hung loosely, and his little red eyes turned hungrily on the strips of good meat hung up to dry.

"Ho! Be seated, friend!" said the old Badger. He lighted and passed the long pipe, while his wife at once broiled a thick slice of savory venison over the coals and offered it to their guest in a wooden basin. The Bear ate like a starving man, and soon after he had eaten he shuffled away.

Next day the Bear came again, and on the day after, and for many days. At each visit he was invited to eat, according to the custom, and feasted well by the Badger, skilful hunter and generous host.

After many days the Bear came one morning looking fat and sleek, and he had brought with him his whole family. Growling savagely, he rudely turned the Badger family out of their comfortable lodge, well stored with good food and soft robes. Even the magic arrows of father Badger were left behind. Crying bitterly, the homeless Badgers went off into the woods to seek another place of shelter. That night they slept cold under a great rock, and the children went supperless to bed, for the Badger could not hunt without his arrows.

All the next day and for several days after he wandered through the forest looking for game, but found none. One night, the children were so hungry and cried so hard, that the poor old father at last said:

" Well, then, I must beg for you! "

So he crept back to his old home, where the Bear family now lived and

grew fat. Standing in the doorway, he
begged quite humbly for a small piece
of meat.

" I would not trouble you," said he,
" but my little folks are starving! "

However, the Bear got up and turned
him angrily out-of-doors, while the ill-
natured little Bears chuckled and laughed
to see how thin and hungry he looked!

All laughed but one, and that one was the smallest and ugliest of the cubs, who had always been teased and abused by the others. He was sorry for the poor Badger, and when no one was looking he slyly stole a piece of his mother's meat and threw it into their hut, and then ran home again.

This happened several times, and now the family of Badgers were only kept from starving by the gifts of the kind-hearted little Bear.

At last came the Avenger, who sprang from a drop of innocent blood. He is very tall, strong and beautiful, and is feared by all wrong-doers. The Bear saw him coming and began to tremble. He at once called to the Badger, who was not far off, and invited him to come and eat.

But the Avenger came first! Then the Bear called upon his wife and children to follow him, and took to his heels. He ran as fast as he could, looking over his shoulder from time to time, for he was really terribly frightened. He never came back any more, and the Badger family returned and joyfully possessed their old home.

There is no meanness like ingratitude.

EIGHTH EVENING
THE GOOD–LUCK TOKEN

EIGHTH EVENING

"AH, Teona, I saw you out to-day with your new bow and arrows! I hope you have not been hasty to display your skill with the new weapons to the injury of any harmless creature," says old Smoky Day, gravely, as the boy hunter arrives quite out of breath.

"You have been told," he adds, "that the animals long ago agreed to sacrifice their lives for ours, when we are in need of food or of skins for garments, but that we are forbidden to kill for sport alone."

"Why, grandfather," the boy admits, "I followed a gray squirrel from tree to tree, and shot at him more than once, but he always dodged the arrow in time!"

"And were you then hungry? did you have any use for the little fellow if you had killed him?" the old man persists. "There was once a squirrel who made a treaty of peace with a little boy like you. I will tell you his story to-night."

THE GOOD-LUCK TOKEN

There was once an old couple who lived quite alone with their little grandson in the midst of a great wood.

They were wretchedly poor, for the old man was now growing too weak to hunt, and often came home at night empty-handed. The old woman dug roots and gathered berries for food; but alas! her eyesight was no longer good, and there were sometimes whole days when there was nothing in the lodge to eat.

One day the boy became very hungry, and he said to his grandfather:

" Grandfather, only make me a bow and some arrows, and I will hunt for us all! "

The first time he went out into the forest with his bow and arrows he met with a Chickadee, who said to him:

" Shoot me! I am willing to give my life to satisfy your hunger."

The boy shot and took home the tiny bird, and when he threw it down before his grandmother it was no longer a Chickadee, but a fine, fat Partridge, and the poor old folks were overcome with joy.

" Ah, ah, my grandson! " they cried. " You are indeed a hunter! "

The next day, when he went out to hunt, the boy walked a long way without seeing any game. At last he thought he heard somebody laughing in the depths of the forest.

The laughter sounded nearer and nearer as he walked on. By and by he was sure he heard some person talking to himself, and in the end he could actually make out the words, although he saw no one.

" Ha, ha," chirrupped the gay voice, " I am surely the luckiest creature alive! I leap and flit all day long from bough to bough. I am quick as a flash, so that I can easily escape my enemies. In my free and happy life there is but one thing I fear, and that is a boy's blunt-headed arrow! "

When the boy heard this, he advanced boldly, and his quick eyes made out a snug wigwam in the hollow of a great tree. He peeped in, and saw that the house was warm and well stored with nuts of all kinds. Its little owner sat flirting his bushy tail in the corner, upon a bed of dry leaves; but as soon as he spied the boy, he ran past him with a scream of fright and scampered off among the thick woods.

The boy followed as fast as he could, and after a long chase he tired out and overtook the Squirrel, who sat coughing and grunting upon the bough of a tree just above his head.

" Boy," he exclaimed, " only spare my life, and you shall have a charm that will make you a successful hunter as long as you live!"

The boy agreed, and the Squirrel took him back to his own wigwam, where he filled the little fellow's bag with nuts from his pile.

" These," said he, " are all lucky nuts, and if you put one of them in your pouch when you go out to hunt, you will surely kill a Bear!"

This the boy did, and to the great joy of the poor old folks he became a famous hunter, so that from that time on they never wanted meat in their lodge.

Do not harm your weaker brothers, for even a little Squirrel may be the bearer of good fortune!

NINTH EVENING

UNKTOMEE AND HIS BUNDLE OF SONGS

NINTH EVENING

"NOW, my grandchildren," says Smoky Day, "I shall tell you of one who is well known in the wonder-world of our people. He is a great traveller, seems to know everybody, and is always good-natured, but he is also a shameless boaster and plays many tricks upon those he meets on the road. No one is so wise and cunning as Unktomee, the Spider; and yet he likes to appear as simple and innocent as a child!

"His adventures are many. Sometimes he gets the better of the animal people, and again they may succeed in outwitting him, so that he is well laughed at for his trouble! We may all learn from these stories of Unktomee and his sly tricks how to be on our guard against those deceitful ones who come to us in the guise of friends."

UNKTOMEE AND HIS BUNDLE OF SONGS

It was a bright, sunshiny day, and the flocks of Ducks flying northward had all stopped to rest beside a little lake, and were splashing and paddling about in the cool water. They were happy and very noisy, but suddenly they ceased their cries and calls and became quite silent, for a queer figure was seen coming toward them along the curve of the beach. It was the figure of a strange little old man, bent nearly double under a huge load of something that looked like dry grass.

" Quack, quack!" said one of the boldest of the Ducks, as the old man drew near with his burden. "What have you there?"

"Oh, that is only a bundle of old songs," replied Unktomee with a smile;

for it was that sly one, that maker of mischief!

Thereupon the Ducks took courage, and quacked and fluttered all about him, crying:

"Sing us an old song, Unktomee!"

Willingly Unktomee threw down his load upon the lake shore, and with the utmost good nature began to build a

little teepee of sticks, thatching it with
the dry grass. In a few minutes it was
done, and he kindly invited the ducks
to enter.

With rustling wings and shining feathers they crowded into the little teepee
until it could hold no more.

Unktomee was there, too. He stayed
by the door, and began to sing:

> "Ishtogmus wachee po!
> Tuwa etowan kin
> Ishtah ne sha kta!
>
> (Dance with your eyes shut!
> Whoever looks shall have red eyes!)"

Every one of the foolish Ducks shut his
eyes tight, and Unktomee, as he sang,
quietly seized one after another by the
neck as they danced in a ring around
the teepee, wrung their necks quickly
and cast them behind them. Not one
had a chance to squawk, so cleverly was

the work done, and there would soon have been none to listen to the old songs!

But after a little a small Duck slyly opened his eyes, and saw Unktomee wringing the necks of his friends.

" Fly! Fly! " he exclaimed in terror. " He is killing us all! "

So all the Ducks that were left alive rose up with a mighty rush of wings and a loud clamor of voices. The grass teepee fell to pieces, and the lucky ones flew away; but lying on the ground beside Unktomee were enough fat Ducks for a fine feast!

And the little Duck that peeped forever after had red eyes!

The children liked this story very much, but it was shorter than usual.

" Tell us about the feast! " they cried. " Tell us about the feast of Unktomee! " So old Smoky Day began again:

Now Unktomee wished to make a feast. The first thing he did was to stand and cry aloud:

"Chagah aoo po-o-o! (Somebody bring me a kettle!)"

He called and called for a long time. At last somebody appeared with the kettle. It was the Fox, who was carrying it in his mouth. Unktomee thanked him carelessly, and after waiting awhile, the Fox went sadly away again.

Then Unktomee dressed the Ducks whose necks he had wrung, built a fire, fetched water and put them on to boil. But he was tired as well as hungry, and while his dinner was cooking, he thought he might as well take a nap. So he lay down in the warm sand near by, first telling his Face to be on the watch and to twitch if any one came, so as to awaken him.

While Unktomee slept, the Fox re-

turned with a friend. Unktomee's Face
did not twitch as it had been told to do,
for the Foxes stroked it very gently,
and told it to be quiet. Having done this,
they quietly ate every bit of the rich
meat, and put the bones back into the
pot.

When at last Unktomee yawned and
awoke, he was very hungry indeed. He
looked to see whether his dinner was
ready, and found nothing in the kettle
except bones!

" Ah! the Ducks have boiled too long,"
he said to himself. " The meat will
all be in the bottom of the pot."

When he discovered that the bones
had been picked clean, he was very
angry, and scolded his Face severely
for not awakening him in time.

*He who deceives others may himself be
caught some day.*

TENTH EVENING
UNKTOMEE AND THE ELK

TANAGELA AND HER LITTLE BROTHER.

TENTH EVENING

"TELL us another story of Unktomee, grandfather!" cry several of the children, as soon as they are inside the old story-teller's wigwam on the tenth evening.

"Ah, I thought you would ask for another!" remarks the old man with quiet satisfaction. "There are many stories of his dealings with the animal people. He loves to go among them and even to take their shape, that he may make fools of them the more easily. This may do very well for a time, but it is generally not long before he is ready to cry 'Enough!'"

UNKTOMEE AND THE ELK

It was midsummer, and the Elk people were feasting in great numbers upon the slopes of the mountain. Sleek, fat and handsome, they browsed hither and thither off the juicy saplings and rich grass, drank their fill from the clear mountain streams, and lay down to rest at their ease in the green shade through the heat of the day.

Unktomee, who had been travelling far and was hungry and foot-sore, looked upon them with envy.

" Ah," said he to himself, " that is the life for me! Surely these are the happiest people on earth, for they have all things in abundance and are so fleet of foot that they need fear no danger! "

Accordingly, he hid his bow and quiver full of arrows in a hollow tree, with all of his clothing and other weapons, so that

he might appear quite naked and harm-
less before the timid Elk people. They
saw that he was unarmed, and they
stood still as he approached.

"Here comes Unktomee," said they
doubtfully to one another.

"Ah, brothers!" he pleaded with them,
"you have enough; you are at peace
with the tribes; you overlook the valley
and all its dwellers are below you! None
is so happy as you. Will you not make
me one of you?"

"Friend!" exclaimed their leader,
"you do not know what you ask! To
be sure, it is now midsummer; our
clothing and our weapons are new, there
is food in plenty, and we may seem to be
happy. However, our antlers, our only
weapons, are yet soft, and the Wolf and
the Wild Cat are ready and fearless to attack us. Our only hope of escape is in
our fleetness, since we are watched all day

by the cruel eyes of those who live upon flesh, of whom the most dangerous of all is Man!"

" I know all this," replied Unktomee. " Others may have stronger weapons than you, but I see none with your beauty, your stately height, your freedom and ease of life. I beg of you to allow me to share it!"

" If you can pass the test, we will admit you," they said at last. " Notice our eyes — we must be ever watchful; our ears — they are constantly on guard! Can you smell an enemy even against the wind? Can you detect his footfall before he is near?"

Unktomee passed the test and was finally admitted to the company of the Elks; in fact, he was made the chief of them all, for such he wanted to be.

" Now," said they, " we have made you our leader. You must guide us so that we shall be safe from the hunters!"

Proud of his long limbs and of his stately antlers, he led them all down the hill, running back now and then to urge the hindermost ones into line. When they stopped to rest, he lay down a little apart from the others, under a spreading oak.

Suddenly they all sprang up and fled, for Unktomee had cried out to them:

"Fly! fly! I am struck by an arrow!"

But when no hunter appeared, they were provoked, and grumbled among themselves:

"Unktomee is deceiving us; it was only a stick that fell from the tree!"

Then they all lay down a second time, and a second time the Elks were aroused in vain. They were still more displeased, and said to one another:

" It was only an acorn that fell upon him while he slept! "

A third time they lay down, but this time the Elks stole away from Unktomee and left him sleeping, for they had scented the hunter. When the hunter came, therefore, he found only the chief Elk still sleeping, and he let fly an arrow and wounded him severely.

Unktomee was now in great fear and pain, and he bitterly regretted that he had become an Elk, for he had learned that their life is full of anxiety. The Elks had taught him that it is well to be content with our own, for there is no life that is free from hardship and danger.

ELEVENTH EVENING
THE FESTIVAL OF THE LITTLE PEOPLE

ELEVENTH EVENING

"YOU are late to-night, my grand-children," grumbles the good old wife of Smoky Day, as she stands in front of her low doorway, peering under the folds of her dark blanket at the little toiling figures slowly coming nearer, and the many twinkling lights across the snow.

"My mother gave a feast to-day," murmurs Tanagela, in her soft voice. "There were so many people for us to serve — I could not come any sooner! But see, grandmother! I have brought you some boiled rice and venison," she ends, proudly bringing out the heavy kettle from under her skin robe as they enter the well-smoked lodge.

" Ah, ah! " exclaims the story-teller,
whose old eyes brighten at the sight of
the good food. " We are to feast to-
night, it seems; therefore I shall tell
you of a feast and what came after."

THE FESTIVAL OF THE LITTLE PEOPLE

The big voice of the Bumble-Bee was
heard in every nook and corner of the
wood, and from end to end of the deep
valley, for Unktomee, the generous, was
giving a feast, and the Bee was his
herald, the crier of the day.

" Ho, every creeper, every buzzer,
all ye little people who fly without
feathers, come this day to the festival! "
boomed the Bee. " All must prepare to
exhibit their best skill; the Toad, who
can neither fly nor run, his brother the
Bullfrog, with his band of musicians,
and even the Flying-squirrel with the
rest. Tanagela, the Humming-bird, will

be the judge of beauty, and the Bat will judge your skilful performance in the air. That wise medicine-man, the Serpent, will also be there!"

So Unktomee's herald made the cedar-fringed gulches and pine-scented hill-tops fairly hum with his call.

It was in July, the Moon of Black Cherries, and the Little People gathered in great numbers at the place of the Singing Waterfall, which had been chosen for the meeting-place. The happy valley buzzed with their million voices.

Then Unktomee, the prudent, saw fit to appoint certain warriors to keep order at the festival. For many were present, therefore mishap or injustice might be.

The Wolf was ordered to watch upon the surrounding hills, so that no enemy should come near; and the Owl was appointed to keep order within the camp, and especially to see that neither the Bat, the Night-hawk nor the Swallow tribe were permitted to disturb the little insect people.

The day opened well, with a chorus of praise from the great orchestra — a sunrise song, opened by Ta-she-ya-ka, the Meadow-lark, in which even the crickets joined, with their slender instruments.

Then came the contest of beauty, in which the Butterflies, in their gauzy dresses of every color, won the first prize. The Bat, however, who was to judge of feats on the wing, had slyly made a meal of some of the lesser contestants. The Owl swooped down upon him to punish him, and there was great confusion.

Unktomee could do nothing with his guests. The Toad began to devour the smaller creepers, the Snake attacked the Toad, and even the Wolf came down from his station on the hills to make a raid upon the helpless Little People. Thus began the warfare and preying among these feeble tribes that has lasted to this day.

It is not wise to put the strong in authority over the weak.

TWELFTH EVENING
EYA THE DEVOURER

TWELFTH EVENING

"WE shall hear to-night of one good deed done by Unktomee," begins the old teacher, when all are in their places. "In the old days, longer ago than any one can remember, no one was more feared and dreaded than Eya, the Glutton, the devouring spirit that went to and fro upon the earth, able to draw all living creatures into his hideous, open mouth! His form was monstrous and terrifying. No one seemed to know what he feared, or how he might be overcome. Whole tribes of people were swallowed up by him, and there was no help!

"At last came Unktomee, and by his quick wit and genial ways got the better of this enemy of our race. He is very hard to kill, for he often comes to life again after he has been left for dead. Perhaps by Eya is meant the terrible hunger, or the sickness that runs like fire from lodge to lodge and sweeps away whole villages."

EYA THE DEVOURER

Once upon a time, an old woman who was gathering wood found a lost babe deep in the forest, and bringing him to the camp, gave him to the chief's pretty daughter. The girl, who was very tender-hearted, took the child and cared for him as her own.

She fed **him** often, but he was never satisfied and continually cried for more. When he screamed, his mouth stretched from ear to ear, and far down his red throat she seemed to see a great company of people struggling in confusion. However, she told no one, but patiently tended the strange child and carried him about with her everywhere.

At dead of night, when all in the lodge were asleep, the tender-hearted maiden was aroused by the crying of her babe. As she bent over him, there seemed to come from his wide-open mouth, as if from the depths of the earth, the far-off voices of many people in distress.

Then at last she went and awoke the chief, her father, and said to him:

" Father, come and listen to the voice of my babe! "

He listened for a moment and exclaimed in horror:

" My child, this is Eya, he who devours all things, even whole villages! This that we hear is. the crying of the people whom he has swallowed. Now he has taken the form of an innocent babe and is come to destroy us!

"We must steal away quietly while he sleeps, and travel fast and far before morning."

In whispers they aroused the sleeping people, and all broke camp without disturbing the child, who once more slept in the chief's teepee, which they left still standing.

All night they travelled at their best pace, and when morning came, they had come to a wide and deep river. Here Unktomee, the crafty one, came to meet them, smiling and rubbing his hands.

When he had learned what caused the people of a whole village to flee in the night, he kindly offered to help them against their powerful enemy. Terrified though they were, they were even then unwilling, for they feared lest he might play some trick upon them; but Unktomee persisted, and went back upon their trail to meet the Devourer.

He had not gone far before he saw Eya hastening after the fleeing ones, his ugly mouth gaping widely and his great, unwieldy body supported by a pair of feeble legs that tottered under its weight.

" Where are you going, younger brother? " asked Unktomee, pleasantly.

" How dare you call me younger brother? " angrily returned the other. " Do you not know that I was the first one created upon the solid earth? "

" If that is so, I must be older than you," replied Unktomee, in his good-natured way, " for I was created upon the face of the water, before the dry land itself! I know whom you seek, younger brother, and am come out to help you.

" Those foolish ones whom you are

following are encamped on the river close at hand, and I will lead you to them presently. They cannot escape you. Why not rest a little now, and refresh yourself with the delicacy that I have prepared for you? See, these are human ears, nicely dried for your meal!"

So saying, Unktomee pointed to a great heap of mussel shells that lay upon the hill-top. The greedy monster was deceived, and hastily swallowed the shells, which caused him such distress that he was helpless, and was easily dispatched by the men of the village, who now came out to kill him. No sooner had they cut open his enormous body with their knives, than a large company of people issued forth upon the plain, and began dancing and singing songs of praise for their deliverance.

THIRTEENTH EVENING
THE WARS OF WA-KEE-YAN AND UNK-TAY-HEE

THIRTEENTH EVENING

"WERE you not frightened last night, grandfather?" exclaims Waola, the boldest of the boys, before the little circle has fairly settled into quiet. "Thunder in the Moon of Sore Eyes is not heard so often! My little sister cried bitterly, and Uncle says that it is an omen of misfortune."

"So it would have seemed to me once, my grandson," replies the old sage, with his pleasant smile. "But I am an old man, and I have heard the Thunder-Bird speak even more loudly, both in season and out of season, yet no evil came of it to our people. Truly I think that the Great Mystery has set bounds to the terrors of these his warriors, so that we need not tremble before them as in the old days, when their laws were not fully known.

" There is a very old story concerning these matters, which I will tell you to-night."

THE WARS OF WA-KEE-YAN AND UNK-TAY-HEE

Wa-kee-yan is the Great Bird of storm and tempest, who was appointed in the beginning of things to keep the earth and also the upper air pure and clean. Although there is sometimes death and destruction in his path, yet he is a servant of the Great Mystery and his work is good.

Yet he rules only one half the year. The other half is ruled by Wa-zee-yah, the Spirit of Cold, and he too purifies the air and the water.

When Wa-zee-yah, the North Wind, the Cold-Maker, comes, the animals put on thicker robes and some even change their color to be like the white blanket that he lays over the earth.   Then the waters are imprisoned for a season, and all things sleep and rest.

Then comes He-yo-kah, the South-Wind, also called the Fool-Wind, he who is the herald of the Thunder-Bird and causes all the trees and the plains to put on their garments of green.

For ages there had been war between the Thunder-Bird, the ruler of the upper air, and the Water Monster, or Unk-tay-hee, the ruler of the deep.   Whenever a black cloud appeared in the sky and cast its threatening shadow upon the water, all the fishes knew it for a warning to descend to the floor of their watery abode, the deep, dark realm, away from the power of his arrows.

Even the sea birds must seek their sheltered coves and hiding-places, pull tight their downy blankets and be still, for now Wa-kee-yan would sweep sea and air with his mighty wing, and punish the disobedient.

All was quiet before his approach. His breath was the tempest, the roll of the thunder his drum-beat, the lightning's flash his tomahawk. At his approach, the face of the deep was thrown into a mighty commotion. Column after column of white warriors advanced boldly upon the land, and broke upon the rocky shores with a loud war-whoop. Such was the combat of the Spirits of Air and Water, at which all living creatures hid themselves and trembled.

At last the great peace-maker, the Sun, appeared, holding in his hand the Rainbow, like a flag of many colors, a sign that the battle is over. He sent each of the warriors to his own place. Gentle airs came down from above to meet and play with the little waves that danced upon the blue water. He who is our Father, the father of our bodies, whose wife is our Mother the Earth, wishes safety and peace for all his children, therefore he still watches the unruly ones from the middle of the sky, and their battles are quickly ended.

FOURTEENTH EVENING

THE LITTLE BOY MAN

FOURTEENTH EVENING

" I SHALL now tell you of the First Man, and how he came upon earth as an infant, yet without father or mother. Listen well, my children, for you should never forget this story."

THE LITTLE BOY MAN

At the beginning of things, He-who-was-first-Created found himself living alone. The earth was here before him, clothed in green grass and thick forests, and peopled with the animal tribes. Then all these spoke one language, and the Lonely One was heralded by them everywhere as he roamed to and fro over the world, both upon dry land and in the depths of the sea.

One day, when he returned to his teepee from a long wandering, he felt a pain in his left foot, and lo! a splinter in the great toe! Drawing out the splinter, he tossed it upward through the smoke-hole of the lodge. He could hear it roll and rattle down over the birch-bark covering, and in the instant that it touched the ground, there arose the cry of a new-born child!

He-who-was-first-Created at once came forth and took up the infant, who was the Boy Man, the father of the human race here upon earth.

Now the little Boy Man grew and flourished, and was perfectly happy under the wise guidance of his friend and Elder Brother. Although he had neither father nor mother, and only animals for playmates, it is said that no child born of human parents has ever led so free and happy a life as he. In those days, there was peace between the animals and the Boy Man. Sometimes they challenged him to friendly contests, whereupon He-who-was-first-Created taught his little brother how to outwit them by clever tricks and devices. This he was often able to do; but not always; for sometimes the animals by their greater strength finally overcame him.

One morning the Boy Man went out from his lodge as usual to the day's occupations, but did not return at night nor for many nights afterward. He-who-was-first-Created mourned and wailed long for the lost one. At last he became angry, and set out to look for the bones of his brother.

He travelled from east to west across the world, but found no trace of the one he sought, and all of the land creatures whom he questioned declared that they had not seen him pass by.

Next he followed the rivers, and the shores of the Great Lakes, and there one day he heard an old woman singing as she cut down a tree at the edge of the water. The traveller came closer to hear the words of the song; and lo! it was a song of the scalp-dance, and in it she spoke the name of the lost Boy Man.

He-who-was-first-Created now turned himself into a King-fisher, and so approached unsuspected and talked with the old Beaver-woman. From her he learned that his younger brother had been enticed into the Great Water and destroyed by the monster of the deep, Unk-tay-hee. Thereupon he went down to the shore and changed himself into a tall pine overlooking the lake.

For many moons He-who-was-first-Created remained thus, until at last he beheld two huge forms rising up in the midst of the waves. The monsters

glided gradually toward the shore and
lay basking in the sun at his feet, rock-
ing gently with the motion of the quiet

water. It was old Unk-tay-hee and his
mate.

"Husband!" exclaimed the wife of
Unk-tay-hee, "for ages this has been
our resting-place, and yet I have never
seen this tree before!"

"Woman, the tree has always been
there!" returned the water monster.

"But I am sure it was not here before," she insisted.

Then Unk-tay-hee wound his immense scaly tail about the giant pine and tried to pull it out by the roots. The water foamed and boiled with his struggles, but He-who-was-first-Created stood firm, and at last the monster gave up the attempt.

"There," he declared, "I told you it had always been there!" His wife appeared satisfied, and presently the gentle waves rocked them both to sleep.

Then He - who - was - first - Created returned to his own shape, and with his long spear he stabbed each of the monsters, so that with groans of pain they dove down to their homes at the bottom of the great lake, and the waters boiled above them, and the foam was red with their blood.

FIFTEENTH EVENING
THE RETURN OF THE LITTLE BOY MAN

FIFTEENTH EVENING

GRANDFATHER has scarcely taken up his long pipe to-night before the children begin to gather, impatient for the end of the story. Chatanna has been begging his father to tell him whether the Little Boy Man was ever found, but he has been obliged to wait for the old man to go on with his tale.

THE RETURN OF THE LITTLE BOY MAN

He-who-was-first-Created now took the form of a swallow, and flew down from the high cliffs, skimming over the surface of the water. Within a sheltered cove among the pines, the water-birds were holding a feast. Some were singing, some dancing, and that great medicine-man, the Loon, was among them, blowing his sacred whistle.

The Lonely One in the form of a swallow dipped down to the water's edge and addressed the Loon respectfully, asking for some of the secrets of his medicine. The Loon was very kind. He taught him several mystery songs, and showed him how to treat the sick.

"Now," said the Swallow, "if you will permit me to take your form for a short time, I will go down into the deep and try to cure Unk-tay-hee and his wife of their dreadful wounds!"

The Loon made no objection, so the new-made conjurer balanced himself upon the crest of a wave and gave his loudest call before he dove down, down into the blue water! There in the watery world the people saw him as it were sailing down from the sky. His path led now through a great forest of sea weeds, now upon the broad plains, and finally he came into a deep valley of the under-world, where he found everybody anxiously waiting for him. He was met by the old Turtle, who begged him to make haste, for the chief and his wife were in great agony.

" Let all the people retire, for I must be alone in order to work a cure," declared the supposed medicine-man, as he entered the teepee of the water monster.

All went away unwillingly — the Turtle last of all. He told the others that he had heard the great conjurer whisper as his hand touched the door-flap: " Ah, my poor brother! " Now this door-flap was made from the skin of the little Boy Man.

He-who-was-first-Created, when he was

inside the lodge, paid no attention to the dreadful groans of the monsters, but at once took down the skin of his brother, and as he did so, he saw the little Water-snake spying at him from behind the door-way. The others, who were suspicious, had sent him as a scout to see what the medicine-man was doing.

He called the Snake inside, and compelled him to tell where he should find the bones of his brother. Then for a reward he painted the Snake green, and declared that as he had served both sides, he should crawl upon his belly forever after.

He-who-was-first-Created gathered up all the bones and took them with him to dry land. There he immediately built a fire and heated stones for the first sweat lodge. He also picked a bunch of sage-brush, and fetched water in a large shell.

Having carefully wrapped the bones with the dry skin of his brother and built over them a low shelter of willow withes, he covered the lodge tightly with green boughs and then thrust in his right arm and began to sprinkle water with the bunch of sage upon the heated stones.

The steam arose and filled the lodge, and with the steam there came a faint sighing sound.

A second time he sprinkled water, and there were rustlings within as if the dry bones were gathering themselves together.

When he put in his hand for the third time he could hear a sound like far-off singing. Immediately after the Little Boy Man spoke in his own voice, begging to be let out of the lodge.

SIXTEENTH EVENING
THE FIRST BATTLE

SIXTEENTH EVENING

"THIS is a very long story that I am telling you," declares Smoky Day, "and many evenings will not see the end of it. There are some adventures of the Little Boy Man that must wait for another winter. To-night I will tell you how it happened that the old friendship was broken between man and the animal people."

THE FIRST BATTLE

Now after some time it came about that the animals became jealous of the greater wit of the Boy Man, and as they feared that he would somehow gain the mastery over them, they began secretly to plot against him.

At about the same time the Boy Man began to question his Elder Brother, and to ask him:

"Brother, why have all these people weapons, such as spears upon their heads and daggers in their mouths, while I am unarmed and naked?"

Then He-who-was-first-Created replied sadly:

"My younger brother, the time is now come to give you weapons and I am sorry for it. Now at last there is war in the hearts of the animals and of man; but they are many and you are only one, therefore I shall help you!"

Then he gave him a strong bow and arrows with flint heads, also a spear with head of stone, and showed him how to use them.

Afterward he tossed a pebble into the air, and it came down as a wall of rock, enclosing their dwelling. He tossed up

another and another, until they were de-
fended by high cliffs on every side.
Upon the flat tops of the cliffs he spread
out the new weapons, whose stone heads
were destined to be scattered far and
wide when the battle should be over,
to be sought out and preserved by men
as relics of the beginning of warfare.

The first battle was announced by a
single Buffalo-bull, running at top speed
over the prairie. This messenger as-
signed to each his part in the attack.
The Beaver was ordered to dam the
streams, and the Badger to dig trenches
under the defences of the Boy Man, so
that they might flood his dwelling.

The Rabbits, Squirrels and other feeble
folk were to gather food for the warriors,
of whom the principal ones were the
Bear, Wolf, Wildcat and Bison. The
Swallow served as messenger to the birds,
and the swift Trout carried the news to

the finny tribes, for all were to join in this war.

With the gray dawn came the Wolf's long howl, the first war-whoop, breaking the silence and peace of the world.

When the sun rose, dancing for an instant upon the sharp edge of the sky, one after another all of the animals joined in the great war-cry, with bellowings and screechings of the larger beasts, the barking of Wolves, the hissing of Snakes, and the shrill cries of the feathered ones, of whom the Crane and the Loon were loudest.

The Boy Man stood erect on the top of the wall, and saw the warriors coming from all directions, as far as the eye could reach. On they came, with a mighty thunder of hoofs and a trampling of many feet! Overhead that great war-chief of the air, the Eagle, commanded his winged forces, while from below the

creepers and crawlers began to scale the
lofty defences of the Boy Man.   There
he stood alone, and fearlessly let fly
hundreds of sharp arrows, of which every
one found its mark, until the ground
was choked with the fallen.

Presently there descended upon him
great hosts of the smaller winged people,
who also had been provided with sharp
and poisonous weapons.   Against these
his Elder Brother had forgotten to warn
him; but now he was told in haste to
strike two flints together and to catch
the spark that should come in the dry
fallen leaves.   Soon a great cloud of
smoke and flames arose toward heaven,
not only driving off the little winged
warriors, but forcing the whole body
of the enemy to retreat in confusion,
for they had never seen fire before, and
to this day it is feared by all and used
by man only.

Thus the animals were convinced that Man is their master. When they sued for peace, all agreed to give him of their flesh for food and their skins for clothing, while he on his side promised never to kill any wantonly. The Boy Man further agreed that they might keep their weapons to use in their own defence. This was the first treaty made upon earth.

SEVENTEENTH EVENING
THE BELOVED OF THE SUN

SEVENTEENTH EVENING

" GRANDFATHER, is not the night beautiful after the long storm? " whispers Tanagela shyly. " The moon always seems to me like a beautiful woman, for she often hides her round, shining face with a blanket of cloud, and sometimes she even runs away from us altogether, as if she were tired or displeased. But to-night she smiles and uncovers her face, so that all the young men are out, each playing upon his flute near the home of the loved one! "

The little maid does not often make so long a speech, and she too hides her face as she comes to the end. But Grandfather smiles indulgently upon his favorite, as he answers:

" And did you not know, then, that she is a woman, my granddaughter? Truly it is time that I told you of these things!"

THE BELOVED OF THE SUN

There was once a man and his wife and two children who had gone away from the rest of the tribe and were living by themselves. One day the man went out hunting as usual, but evening came and he did not return. The next day his wife went to look for him, and neither did she come back to the lodge.

Thus it came about that the young brother and sister were left alone, but they were not unhappy. The boy was a strong and well-grown lad, and he brought home abundance of meat, while the girl cooked his food, tanned the skins and made all of their moccasins and clothing.

They had been living thus for many moons, when very early one morning, soon after her brother had left her for the hunt, the girl's eyes were dazzled by a sudden flash of light, and at the same instant a tall and beautiful young man entered the lodge. She thought at first that her brother had come back, so great was the likeness; but he did not act like him, for his manner was that of a suitor. He remained for some time, but left before the brother returned.

Now the young man saw at once that his sister seemed to be troubled and embarrassed about something. He questioned her, and she hung her head in silence. Three times this happened, and on the third day she told him all.

"To-morrow," said he, "I will set out as usual early in the morning, but I shall not go far. If your visitor comes, keep him until I return."

Accordingly the next day the brother went a little way from home and hid himself in a hollow tree from which he could watch their dwelling. Soon after the girl's lover appeared, he returned to the lodge and at once fell upon the stranger, for he was very angry.

For some time they wrestled together in silence, and neither was able to gain the mastery over the other. Finally, however, the brother felt that he was being overcome, and he cried out:

"Sister, help, help!"

The girl did not know what to do, but she seized her axe and was about to strike one of the young men when he cried out:

"Take care, sister!"

Then she raised her axe against the

other, but he too exclaimed: "Take care, sister!"

She became more and more bewildered, for the two looked so much alike that it was impossible to tell which one was really her brother.

At last, however, she made up her mind to strike at the stranger, but like a flash of light he eluded her and spoke:

"My friend, do not try to resist me any longer! I came not to harm you or this maiden, but to make her my wife! Know that I am the Sun, and she shall be the Moon and rule over the night if she will come with me!"

"Upon this the maiden yielded and went with him," said Grandfather; "but you see that she will not shine every night, for she was only a mortal maiden and is soon wearied. You know we call the Sun our Grandfather and the Moon

Grandmother, and we also believe that the Stars are their children. Some time I shall tell you how a Star, too, loved an earthly maid."

EIGHTEENTH EVENING
WOOD-CHOPPER AND BERRY-PICKER

" **A** LONG time ago," says the old story-teller, " man was nearer the animal people than he is today; they even spoke the same language and seemed to understand one another perfectly. Sometimes he loved and married among them, but his children were not so good and noble as the first man. There was something of the animal in them.

" There are many stories of this sort, but some of them are long and hard to understand. Perhaps you have heard of Tidoona and Tankadoona, the Indoor One and the Outdoor One, in which the little boy is half-brother to a Bear cub and they meet and play together in secret. To-night, however, I will tell you another story."

WOOD-CHOPPER AND BERRY-PICKER

In the old days, when men and animals spoke one language, a young man who had grown tired of living alone set out to look for a wife. He had not travelled far when he came to a stream of clear water which had been dammed to make a small, round pond. On the shore of the pond was a neat, dome-shaped lodge, and just outside the lodge a pretty woman was busily chopping wood.

The young man stood for some time watching her from behind a tree. Being pleased with her looks and especially with her industry, he presently showed himself, and the girl, whose name was Beaver-woman, received him so kindly that in a short time they had decided to marry and go to house-keeping.

When their little boy came, the proud father wished to take him back and show him to his own people, but to this his wife would not consent.

" If you must return," said she, " very well; but we cannot go with you!"

So the young man, who had a great longing to see again the faces of his kinsfolk, left them behind and journeyed to his father's village. He made them a short visit, and then hastened back to his own home.

Alas, there was no home there! The lodge was destroyed, the dam broken, the pond itself gone, the singing brook was only a thin trickle of water, and his wife and son were nowhere to be found!

The unhappy young man lay upon the ground, mourning for his lost wife and little boy, until a handsome young woman dressed all in black came out of the woods. She supposed that he must be faint for want of food, so she brought him sweet roots and berries. When he had eaten, she kindly combed his hair and washed his face, and after he was refreshed, she comforted him with loving words and caresses, so that he soon forgot the Beaver-woman and took her to be his wife.

Together they went to look for a home. The young man chose a beautiful open spot overlooking much country, but his wife, whose name was Berry-Picker, laughed at him, saying:

"Our people never live in such an open place as that!"

She chose a sheltered spot at the foot of the hill, and there they began to hollow out a comfortable dwelling under the upturned roots of an old fallen tree.

When Berry-Picker, the Bear wife, sent her husband out to look for bedding, he brought in much dry grass; but the Bear wife reproved him, saying:

" Why, husband! you expose our home to the eyes of all! "

All about their lodge were bare spots where he had pulled the grass, so they had to find a new place in which to live.

At last the pair were snug and warm for the winter, and as it was now time to go to sleep, they did so, and slept until they were aroused by the barking of a Dog and the footsteps of a hunter on the crisp snow.

The Bear wife struck the roof of her house, and a Partridge flew up out of the snow with a great whirring of wings. The Dog followed the Partridge and the hunter followed the Dog.

When the hunter came for the second time, she started a Rabbit, which drew the Dog away, and he drew away the hunter.

But when he persisted, and came back for the third time, she left her home and ran for her life, leaving her husband to follow as best he could.

He ran on and on, following his wife's tracks in the deep snow, until he came to a little hut where lived an old Bear.

" Where are you going, my son? " inquired the old man.

"Oh," he replied, "I am only travelling for pleasure!"

"Do not try to deceive me," said the old Bear. "I know well whom you seek! Berry-Picker passed this way only yesterday, on her way to rejoin her people."

"And where do her people live?" asked the young husband.

"They live not far away, my son; but be on your guard; they are a deceitful people and will give you much trouble!"

Thanking the old man, he hurried on, and soon came to the village of the Bears. It was a large village, and the people seemed to have plenty to eat and to be very merry, for they were singing and dancing. As the stranger drew near, every young woman in the great camp came running to meet him. They all looked alike, for every one was dressed in glossy black and all were plump and handsome, and they all crowded about him as if to embrace him, crying:

" Welcome home, my husband! "

Now the young man became very angry, for he knew that the Bears were trying to deceive him, and that if he did not know his own wife, they would take his life. He took no notice of any of the young women, but turned his back on the village and went home to his own country.

This story is told for a warning to those who wish to marry among strangers.

NINETEENTH EVENING

THE SON-IN-LAW

NINETEENTH EVENING

"TELL us, grandfather, who is Chanotedah?" bursts out Waola even before the children are fairly seated. "Uncle told me to-day when I was hunting to beware of the Little Man of the Woods, for if I should meet him I might lose my way and never smell the camp fire again! But when I asked where he was to be found, and how I should know him, he only laughed at me and went on making arrows."

"This Chanotedah is indeed a mischievous fellow," explains the good old man. "He is no larger than a three-year-old child, and is covered with hair. His home is in a hollow tree, and his weapons are the brilliantly colored feathers of gay birds. He delights in confusing the lone hunter who is so unlucky as to come upon him in the depths of the forest. That you may know why this little man has a grudge against our race, I will tell you a story."

THE SON-IN-LAW

Once upon a time there was a young girl whose parents had been taken by the enemy, and who lived alone with her elder brother in the forest, without kinsfolk or neighbors. The young man was a clever hunter who provided more than enough for their needs, and the sister kept his lodge in order and his moccasins well mended, so that for a long time they lived happily together without other company.

A day came, however, when the young man wished to go upon a journey and

to see something of the world. He therefore called upon the Little Man of the
Woods, Chanotedah, and begged him to
look after his sister during his absence.
He then took his bow and quiver full of
arrows, and set out to discover strange
countries.

The traveller met with no adventures
until the third day, when he saw several
boys playing outside the entrance to
their dwelling, which appeared to be
merely a cave in the side of a hill.

"Here comes our brother-in-law!"
they cried, and all ran back into the
cave.

The young man was curious to know
what this meant, and he went boldly in.
Opposite the door of the cave there sat a
handsome young woman, while her father
and mother were seated upon either side
of the fire. The old man at once arose
and greeted the stranger.

"Ho, my son-in-law!" he exclaimed; whereupon the old wife served him with food and waited upon him hospitably.

It appeared, however, that the young woman was kindly disposed toward this good-looking youth, for she soon contrived to warn him secretly of her father's intentions toward him.

"When my father takes you hunting with him," she said, "you must take care always to keep behind him. If he tells you to follow any animal, do not do so, but shoot it from where you stand!"

Next day the old man invited his guest to hunt, and by and by they saw a white Marten in the wood.

"Chase it, chase it, son-in-law!" exclaimed the old man, but the youth stood still and killed the creature with an arrow from his quiver. Alas, it was no

DO NOT SHOOT A WHITE DEER WHEN YOU SEE HIM COMING TOWARD YOU

marten, but one of the boys whom he had seen playing outside the cave!

The next day a white Magpie flew across the path, and the old man again called on his guest to follow. He stopped and aimed an arrow instead, which pierced the second boy to the heart.

" Do not shoot a white Deer when you see him coming toward you," begged the girl of her lover on the third morning, for she wished to save her youngest brother's life. The young man spared the Deer, and the last of the boys came home unhurt; but he himself remembered her warning and took care to keep behind, so that the old man had no chance to kill him.

" Ah, my son-in-law, you have beaten me! Take my daughter; she is now your wife," he said to the young man, who thereupon took his wife home to his own lodge, and his brother-in-law whose life he had spared he took with them to be husband to his sister.

The Little Man of the Woods had guarded the girl safely, but meanwhile he had fallen in love with her and desired to marry her. Being refused, he went away angry and hid in a hollow tree, where he still lives, and all who walk alone in the forest fear to meet him, for he wishes nothing so much as to do a mischief to the descendants of the sister and brother.

TWENTIETH EVENING

THE COMRADES

" THERE is another bad character of whom we have all heard, and some of us have met him," begins the teacher. " His name tells you what he is. He has two faces; one he shows at first when he wishes to be agreeable and has some object to gain; but as soon as he is found out he turns the ugly, scowling face upon you.

" Remember, children, you should not keep two faces — a pleasant one for strangers and a cross face to show when you are at home! Try to imitate the heroes of old, the great and good and helpful, such as the Stone Boy, the Star Boy, the Avenger, he who wears the White Plume, and he who shot the Red

Eagle! If I should be spared to live another winter, I will tell you of them all. To-night we will hear the pleasant story of Mashtinna and his brother-friend."

THE COMRADES

Mashtinna, the Rabbit, was a handsome young man, and, moreover, of a kind disposition. One day, when he was hunting, he heard a child crying bitterly, and made all haste in the direction of the sound.

On the further side of the wood he found one tormenting a baby boy with whips and pinches, laughing heartily meanwhile and humming a mother's lullaby.

"What do you mean by abusing this innocent child?" demanded the Rabbit; but the other showed a smiling face and replied pleasantly:

"You do not know what you are talking about! The child is fretful, and I am merely trying to quiet him."

Mashtinna was not deceived, for he had guessed that this was Double-Face, who delights in teasing the helpless ones.

"Give the boy to me!" he insisted; so that Double-Face became angry, and showed the other side of his face, which was black and scowling.

"The boy is mine," he declared, "and if you say another word I shall treat you as I have treated him!"

Upon this, Mashtinna fitted an arrow to the string, and shot the wicked one through the heart.

He then took the child on his arm and followed the trail to a small and poor teepee. There lived an old man and his wife, both of them blind and nearly helpless, for all of their children and grandchildren, even to the smallest and last, had been lured away by wicked Double-Face.

" Ho, grandfather, grandmother! I have brought you back the child!" exclaimed the Rabbit, as he stood in the doorway.

But the poor, blind old people had so often been deceived by that heartless Double-Face that they no longer believed anything; therefore they both cried out:

" Ugh, you liar! we don't believe a word you say! Get away with you, do!"

Since they refused to take the child, and it was now almost night, the kind-hearted young man wrapped the boy in his own blanket and lay down with him to sleep. The next morning, when he awoke, he found to his surprise that the child had grown up during the night and was now a handsome young man, so much like him that they might have been twin brothers.

" My friend, we are now comrades for life! " exclaimed the strange youth. " We shall each go different ways in the world, doing all the good we can; but if either is ever in need of help let him call upon the other and he will come instantly to his aid! "

The other agreed, and they set out in opposite directions. Not long after, the Rabbit heard a loud groaning and crying as of some person in great pain. When he reached the spot, he found a man with his body wedged tightly in the forks of a tree, which the wind swayed to and fro. He could not by any means get away, and was in great misery.

" I will take your place, brother! " exclaimed the generous young man, upon which the tree immediately parted, and the tree-bound was free. Mashtinna took his place and the tree closed upon him like a vise and pinched him severely.

The pain was worse than he had supposed, but he bore it as long as he could without crying out. Sweat beaded his forehead and his veins swelled to bursting; at last he could endure it no longer, and called loudly upon his comrade to help him. At once the young man appeared and struck the tree so that it parted and Mashtinna was free.

He kept on his journey until he spied a small wigwam quite by itself on the edge of a wood. Lifting the door-flap, he saw no one but an old blind man, who greeted him thankfully.

" Ho, my grandson! you see me, I am old and poor. All the day I see no one. When I wish to drink, this raw-hide lariat leads me to the stream near by. When I need dry sticks for my fire, I follow this other rope and feel my way among the trees. I have food enough, for these bags are packed with dried meat for my use. But alas, my grandson, I am all alone here, and I am blind!"

" Take my eyes, grandfather!" at once exclaimed the kind-hearted young man. " You shall go where you will, and I will remain here in your place."

" Ho, ho, my grandson, you are very good!" replied the old man, and he gladly took the eyes of the Rabbit and went out into the world. The youth stayed behind, and as he was hungry, he ate of the dried meat in the bags.

This made him very thirsty, so he took hold of the raw-hide rope and followed it to the stream; but as he stooped to the brink, the rope broke and Mashtinna fell in.

The water was cold and the bank slippery, but after a hard struggle he got out again and made his way back to the teepee, dripping wet and very miserable. Wishing to make a fire and dry his clothes, he seized the other rope and went to the wood for sticks.

However, when he began to gather the sticks he lost the rope, and being quite blind he did nothing but stumble over fallen logs, and bruise himself against the trunks of trees, and scratch his face among the briers and brambles, until at last he could bear it no longer, and cried out to his comrade to come to his aid.

Instantly the youth appeared and gave him back his eyes, saying at the same time:

" Friend, be not so rash in future! It is right to help those who are in trouble, but one must also consider whether he himself is able to hold out to the end."

TWENTY-FIRST EVENING

THE LAUGH-MAKER

TWENTY-FIRST EVENING

"YOU remember the young man who married among the Bear people," begins Grandfather. "Now to us the Bear seems at times almost human; he can stand and even walk erect; he will cry and groan very like a man when hurt, and there are those who say that he laughs. In the old stories the Bears are a powerful nation; and there is a young man, perhaps the same one I told you of before, who is said to have been living among them at one time with his wife, Woshpee, and their little son."

THE LAUGH-MAKER

The village of the Bears was a large one, and the people were well-fed and prosperous. Upon certain days, a herald went the round of the lodges, announcing in a loud voice that the time had come to " go a-laughing." Not a Bear was left in the village at such times, for every one went, old and young, sick and well, the active and the lame. Only the stranger remained at home, although his wife, Woshpee, always went with her kinsfolk, for somehow he did not feel inclined to " go a-laughing;" and he kept with him his little son, who was half Bear and half human.

One day, however, a curiosity seized him to know what this laughing business might be. He took his boy and followed the Bears at a distance, not choosing to be seen. Their trail led to the shore of the Great Water, and when he had come as near as he could without exposing himself, he climbed a tall pine from whose bushy top he could observe all that took place.

The gathering of the Bears was on a deep bay that jutted inland. Its rocky shores were quite black with them, and as soon as all had become quiet, an old Bear advanced to the water's edge and called in a loud voice:

" E-ha-we-cha-ye-la, e-ha-un-he-pee lo! (Laugh-maker, we are come to laugh!) "

When he had called four times, a small object appeared in the midst of the water and began to swim toward the shore. By and by the strange creature sprawled and clambered out upon a solitary rock that stood partly above the water.

The Laugh-maker was hairless and wrinkled like a new-born child; it had the funniest feet, or hands, or flippers, with which it tried to walk, but only tumbled and flopped about. In the water it was graceful enough, but on dry land so ungainly and ridiculous that the vast concourse of Bears was thrown into fits of hysterical laughter.

" Ha, ha, ha! Waugh, waugh!" they roared, lifting their ugly long muzzles and opening their gaping jaws. Some of them could no longer hold on to the boughs of the trees, or the rocks on which they had perched, and came tumbling down on the heads of the crowd, adding much to the fun. Every motion of the little " Laugh-maker " produced fresh roars of immoderate laughter.

At last the Bears grew weak and helpless with laughing. Hundreds of them sprawled out upon the sand, quite unable to rise. Then the old man again advanced and cried out:

" E-ha-we-cha-ye-la, wan-na e-ha un-ta-pe ktay do! (Laugh-maker, we are almost dead with laughing!)" Upon this the little creature swam back into deep water and disappeared.

Now the stranger was not at all amused and in fact could see nothing to laugh at. When all the Bears had got up and dispersed to their homes he came down from the tree with his little son, and the child wished to imitate his great-grandfather Bear. He went out alone on the sandy beach and began to call in his piping voice:

"Laugh-maker, we are come to laugh!"

When he had called four times, the little creature again showed its smooth black head above the water.

" Ha, ha, ha! Why don't you laugh, papa? It is so funny!" the boy cried out breathlessly.

But his father looked on soberly while the thing went through all its usual antics, and the little boy laughed harder and harder, until at last he rolled and rolled on the sandy beach, almost dead with laughter.

"Papa," he gasped, "if you do not stop this funny thing I shall die!"

Then the father picked up his bow and strung it. He gave one more look at his boy, who was gasping for breath; then he fitted a sharp arrow to the bow and pierced the little Laugh-maker to the heart. He went out and took the skin, and they returned in silence to the camp of the Bears.

Now the next time that the herald called upon the Bears to "go a-laughing," the skin of the Laugh-maker was almost dry, but they knew nothing of it. They went away as usual, and left the young man alone with his son. But he, knowing that his wife's kinsfolk would kill him when they discovered what he had done, took the skin for a quiver and went homeward with his child.

TWENTY–SECOND EVENING

THE RUNAWAYS

TWENTY-SECOND EVENING

" SOME say," remarks Grandfather,
" that the hero of the story I
am about to tell you is the same
as the kind-hearted young man of whom
you heard not long ago — Mashtinna, the
Rabbit. You will remember that he was
uncommonly handsome as well as generous. This time he falls in love, and
there is a wicked old woman in the way;
but you will learn some day that true
love is able to defy and to outwit all its
enemies! "

THE RUNAWAYS

There was once a young man who had
journeyed a long way from home in
search of adventure. One day he came

to a strange village on the border of a great wood, but while yet some distance from the lodges, he happened to glance upward. In the boughs of a tree just above his head he saw a light scaffold, and on the scaffold a maiden sitting at her needle-work.

Instead of boldly entering the village, as he had intended, the youth walked on a little way, then turned and again passed under the tree. He did this several times, and each time he looked up, for the girl was the prettiest that he had ever seen.

He did not show himself to the people, but for several days he lingered on the borders of the wood, and at last he ventured to speak with the maiden and to ask her to be his wife. She did not seem to be at all unwilling; however, she said to him:

" You must be very careful, for my

grandmother does not wish me to marry. She is a very wicked old woman, and has thus far succeeded in killing every one of my suitors."

" In that case, we must run away," the young man replied. " To-night, when your grandmother is asleep, pull up some of the tent-pins and come out. I shall be waiting for you! "

The girl did as he had said, and that same night they fled together and by morning were far from the village.

However, the maiden kept looking over her shoulder as if fearing pursuit, and at last her lover said to her:

" Why do you continue to look behind you? They will not have missed you until daylight, and it is quite certain now that no one can overtake us! "

" Ah," she replied, " my grandmother has powerful magic! She can cover a whole day's journey at one step, and I am convinced that she is upon our trail."

" In that case, you shall see that I too know something of magic," returned the young man. Forthwith he threw down one of his mittens, and lo! their trail was changed to the trail of a Buffalo. He threw down the other mitten, and it became the carcass of a Buffalo lying at the end of the trail.

" She will follow thus far and no farther," he declared; but the maiden shook her head, and ceased not from time to time to glance over her shoulder as they hastened onward.

In truth it was not long till she perceived the old woman in the distance, coming on with great strides and shaking her cane and her gray head at the runaways.

" Now it is my turn!" the girl exclaimed, and threw down her comb, which became a thick forest behind the fleeing ones, so that the angry old woman was held back by the dense underbrush.

When she had come out of the forest at last and was again gaining upon them, the girl threw her awl over her shoulder and it became a chain of mountains with high peaks and sharp precipices, so that the grandmother was kept back longer than before.   Nevertheless, her magic was strong, and she still struggled on after the lovers.

In the meantime, they had come to the bank of a river both wide and deep, and here they stood for a while doubting how they should cross, for there was neither boat nor ford.   However, there were two Cranes near by, and to these the young man addressed himself.

" My friends," said he, " I beg of you to stand on the opposite banks of this river and stretch your necks across, so

that we may cross in safety! Only do
this, and I will give to each of you a
fine ornament for your breast, and long
fringes on your leggings, so that you will
hereafter be called the handsomest of
birds!"

The Cranes were willing to oblige, and

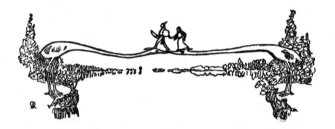

they stood thus with their beaks touching over the stream, so that the lovers
crossed on their long necks in safety.

" Now," exclaimed the young man, " I
must ask of you one more favor! If an
old woman should come down to the river
and seek your help, place your heads
together once more as if to allow her

to cross, but when she is half way over you must draw back and let her fall in mid-stream. Do this, and I promise you that you shall never be in want!"

In a little while the old woman came down to the river, quite out of breath, and more angry than before. As soon as she noticed the two Cranes, she began to scold and order them about.

"Come here, you long-necks, you ungainly creatures, come and help me over this river!" she cried.

The two Cranes again stood beak to beak, but when the wicked grandmother had crossed half way they pulled in their necks and into the water she went, screaming out threats and abuse as she whirled through the air. The current swept her quickly away and she was drowned, for there is no magic so strong that it will prevail against true love.

TWENTY-THIRD EVENING
THE GIRL WHO MARRIED THE STAR

TWENTY-THIRD EVENING

"AH, here is our little Humming-bird, always the first to raise the door-flap!" is the old teacher's pleasant greeting.

"That is because I do not want to lose one word of your good stories, Grandfather," murmurs the little maiden, with her pretty, upward glance and bashful smile.

"I have one for you to-night that ought to please you," he answers thoughtfully. "You know the shining Star people in the heavens above us — you have gazed upon them and doubtless dreamed that you were among them. We believe them to be a higher race than ours. Listen, then, to my story."

THE GIRL WHO MARRIED THE STAR

There were once two sisters who lived alone in an uninhabited place. This was a long time ago, when the tribes upon earth were few, and the animal people were friendly to man. The name of one of the girls was Earth, and the other was called Water.

All their food was brought to them by their animal friends. The Bears supplied them with nuts, berries and wild turnips, and the Bees brought combs dripping with honey. They ate no flesh, for that would be to take life. They dwelt in a lodge made of birch-bark, and their beds were mats woven of rushes.

One clear, summer night the girls lay awake upon their beds, looking up through the smoke-hole of their wigwam and telling one another all their thoughts.

" Sister," said the Earth, " I have seen

a handsome young man in my dreams, and it seemed to me that he came from up yonder!"

"I too have seen a man in my dreams," replied her sister, "and he was a great brave."

"Do you not think these bright stars above us are the sky men of whom we have dreamed?" suggested the Earth.

"If that is true, sister, and it may be true," said the Water, "I choose that brightest Star for my husband!"

"And I," declared her sister, "choose for my husband that little twinkling Star!"

By and by the sisters slept; and when they awoke, they found themselves in the sky! The husband of the elder sister who had chosen the bright star was an old warrior with a shining name, but the husband of the younger girl was a fine-looking young man, who had as yet no great reputation.

The Star men were kind to their wives, who lived very happily in their new home. One day they went out to dig wild turnips, and the old warrior said to his wife:

" When you are digging, you must not hit the ground too hard! "

The younger man also warned his wife, saying:

" Do not hit the ground too hard! "

However, the Earth forgot, and in her haste she struck the ground so hard with the sharp-pointed stick with which she dug turnips, that the floor of the sky was broken and she fell through.

Two very old people found the poor girl lying in the meadow.

They kindly made for her a little wigwam of pine boughs, and brought ferns for her bed. The old woman nursed her as well as she could, but she did nothing but wail and cry.

"Let me go to him!" she begged. "I cannot live without my husband!"

Night came, and the stars appeared in the sky as usual. Only the little twinkling Star did not appear, for he was now a widower and had painted his face quite black.

The poor wife waited for him a long time, but he did not come, because he could not. At last she slept, and dreamed she saw a tiny red Star in the sky that had not been there before.

"Ah!" said she, "that is Red Star, my son!"

In the morning she found at her side a pretty little boy, a Star Boy, who afterward grew to be a handsome young man and had many adventures. His guides by night through the pathless woods were the Star children of his mother's sister, his cousins in the sky.

TWENTY–FOURTH EVENING
NORTH WIND AND STAR BOY

TWENTY-FOURTH EVENING

"HUN, hun, hay! Old man Wazeya, the North Wind, is again on the war-path! You are brave children to come out to-night! See, he shakes his downy feather robe, and the little snow-flakes fly fast and faster! He gives his war-whoop, and cowards seek the safe shelter of their own wigwams. You are no cowards, I am sure of that, so I shall tell you of the battle between Wazeya and one of our great heroes, the son of a mortal maiden and a Star."

NORTH WIND AND STAR BOY

In the very old days at the beginning of things, Star Boy went about the world as a champion, defending all feeble folk against the attacks of their enemies.

The champion was so strong that he could not bend his bow of wood without breaking it, therefore he armed himself with a bone bow, a bone knife and a stone war-club.

One day, he came to the village of the Frogs, who poured out of their lodges to meet him and set before him food, but no water. "He who goes to the water," said they, "never returns. A great warrior lies there who has swallowed many of us alive, and now we are perishing of thirst!"

Star Boy himself was so thirsty that after he had eaten, he went down to the water, and was instantly swallowed by Tamahay, the Pickerel. But with his bone knife he slashed the Pickerel in the gills and escaped; after which he warned the big fish, saying:

STAR BOY ATTACKED BY HINHAN, THE OWL.

" Be careful how you wantonly destroy this people, for some day they will be used to destroy you! "

He then went on his way, as far as another village of Little People, who complained that they had no fire-wood.

" We dare not go to the wood any more," they said, "for there a fierce warrior lives who swoops down from above and devours us! "

Star Boy at once went to the wood, where he was attacked by Hinhan, the Owl. Him he easily conquered with his stone war-club. " Because of your cruelty," he said to the Owl, " the sun shall blind you hereafter, so that you can hunt only in the dark, when the Mouse people are advised to take to their holes and hiding-places."

Now Star Boy travelled northward, until he had reached the very northern-most country, and in that far land he found a people in great distress. This was because they feared Wazeya, the North Wind, who drove away the buffalo herds so that they had no meat. " And when he points his finger at one of us," said they, " that man dies! "

" Come, let us hunt the buffalo! " said Star Boy to them; and although they were starving, they were afraid and unwilling to go. However, he made some of the men go out with him, and upon the open plain they met with North Wind, who at once challenged the champion to do battle. The two rushed upon one another with great fury, and in the first onset Star Boy broke the bow of North Wind; but in the second, Star Boy was overthrown and lay as one dead.

However, after a time he got up again, and they met for the third bout, when lo! neither could prevail against the other, so that in the midst of the fight they were obliged to sit upon a snowbank to rest. Star Boy sat upon his calf-skin and fanned himself with an eagle-wing, and immediately the snow began to melt and the North Wind was forced to retreat. Before he went away, he made a treaty of peace with Star Boy, promising to come to earth for half the year only, and to give timely warning of his approach, so that the people might prepare for his coming and lay up food against the day of scarcity. By this means the winter and summer were established among us.

TWENTY-FIFTH EVENING
THE TEN VIRGINS

TWENTY-FIFTH EVENING

THE strong sun of March still hovers over the deep blue lake, and last night's snow flurry has quite vanished from the pleasant, brown face of our Grandmother Earth, when the children arrive at Smoky Day's wide-open doorway. There is a tang in the air and a stir in the blood to-night that moves the old man to tell a tale of youth and adventure. And this is the tale:

THE TEN VIRGINS

There were once two brothers who loved one maiden, and it appeared that the younger brother was the favorite. One day, the jealous elder invited his brother to go hunting with him upon an island in the great lake, a day's journey in canoes from their village.

No sooner had they touched shore than the elder said:

" Do you go to the other end of the island, and I will drive the Deer toward you! "

The other obeyed; but although he waited a long time on the further side, no Deer appeared, nor did he see anything of his brother. At last he returned through the woods to the spot where they had landed; and behold! the canoe with his brother was almost out of sight on the blue waters of the lake.

The young man, thus abandoned, wandered about the island for many days, living upon the game which he found there in abundance. He had grown very lonely and tired of his solitary life, when one day a strange old man with long, white hair appeared on the shore.

"My son," said he, "you look un-happy! Tell me if there is anything you wish for."

"I want nothing except to cross the water to the mainland," replied the young man, "but I have no boat nor the means of making one."

"Get upon my back, and I will take you over in safety," returned the patriarch. Accordingly he took him upon his back and swam across the lake with his burden.

Now the young man was grateful to his rescuer and he no longer cared to return to his own people and to the brother who had betrayed him, therefore he went with the old man to his wigwam to hunt for him.

One day, when he was out hunting as usual, he thought he heard the far-off, musical sound of girls' laughter from the depths of the forest. He turned in the direction of the sound and soon came upon a broad trail, which he followed until he was overtaken by nine young men, all running eagerly along the same trail.

They at once made him join their company, saying that they had needed just one more to complete their number. The ten hastened on, and presently they overtook ten beautiful young damsels. Night fell, and they all went into camp together on the shore of the great lake.

The girls were very friendly and chatted pleasantly with the young men during the evening, until each party retired to sleep under a hurriedly made arbor of green boughs.

Very early in the morning the youths awoke; but lo! their companions had vanished, and they could see only the flash of a distant paddle where lake met sky at the far-off horizon line.

There was no boat, and they were about to go back in despair, when the

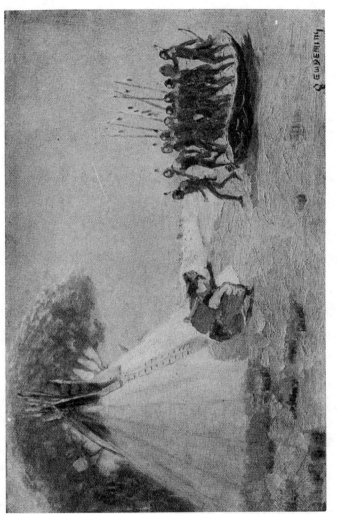

SHE TOOK UP HANDSFUL OF ASHES TO THROW INTO THEIR FACES.

[*Page* 227

young man who had last joined the party
spied a little mussel shell at the edge of
the water, and invited them to step in.
At first they were doubtful and hung
back; but in the end one ventured and
stepped into the shell, which bore up his
weight.   Then another and another followed, until the ten men stood upon the
shell, which had become a fine large
canoe, and carried them all in safety to
the opposite shore.

There they beheld the great white
wigwam in which dwelt the ten virgins
with their grandmother, who was a
wicked old witch.

As soon as she saw the young men she
took up handfuls of ashes to throw into
their faces, and one after another fell
senseless at her feet.

Last of all came the fortunate younger
brother. He had borrowed the weapons
of the old man with whom he lived, and

it chanced that this man was a greater wonder-worker even than the witch. Therefore he had merely turned toward her his magic shield to keep off the shower of ashes, when the old woman lost all her power to hurt, and at once each lusty young man sprang quickly up to claim his bride.

TWENTY-SIXTH EVENING

THE MAGIC ARROWS

TWENTY-SIXTH EVENING

THE wise and old heads among the Indians love children's company, and none is more sorry than Smoky Day when the village breaks up for the spring hunt, and story-telling is over for the season.

" I hope," he says kindly, " that you have listened so well to these tales of our people, and repeated them so often that you will never forget them!"

" We have, grandfather, we have!" they reply in chorus.

" We must not only remember and repeat," he continues, " but we must consider and follow their teachings, for it is so that these legends that have come down to us from the old time are kept

alive by each new generation. There
is much to learn from the story of one who
was so modest that he took the form of a
ragged and homeless little boy, and did
his good deeds in secret."

THE MAGIC ARROWS

There was once a young man who
wanted to go on a journey. His mother
provided him with sacks of dried meat
and pairs of moccasins, but his father
said to him:

" Here, my son, are four magic arrows.
When you are in need, shoot one of them!"

The young man went forth alone, and
hunted in the forest for many days.
Usually he was successful, but a day
came when he was hungry and could not
find meat. Then he sent forth one of the
magic arrows, and at the end of the day
there lay a fat Bear with the arrow in
his side. The hunter cut out the tongue

for his meal, and of the body of the Bear
he made a thank-offering to the Great
Mystery.

Again he was in need, and again in the

morning he shot a magic arrow, and at
nightfall beside his camp-fire he found
an Elk lying with the arrow in his heart.
Once more he ate the tongue and offered

up the body as a sacrifice. The third time he killed a Moose with his arrow, and the fourth time a Buffalo.

After the fourth arrow had been spent, the young man came one day out of the forest, and before him there lay a great circular village of skin lodges. At one side, and some little way from the rest of the people, he noticed a small and poor tent where an old couple lived all alone. At the edge of the wood he took off his clothes and hid them in a hollow tree. Then, touching the top of his head with his staff, he turned himself into a little ragged boy and went toward the poor tent.

The old woman saw him coming, and said to her old man: " Old man, let us keep this little boy for our own! He seems to be a fine, bright-eyed little fellow, and we are all alone."

" What are you thinking of, old woman? " grumbled the old man. " We can hardly keep ourselves, and yet you talk of taking in a ragged little scamp from nobody knows where!"

In the meantime the boy had come quite near, and the old wife beckoned to him to enter the lodge.

"Sit down, my grandson, sit down!" she said, kindly; and, in spite of the old man's black looks, she handed him a small dish of parched corn, which was all the food they had.

The boy ate and stayed on. By and by he said to the old woman: "Grandmother, I should like to have grandfather make me some arrows!"

"You hear, my old man?" said she. "It will be very well for you to make some little arrows for the boy."

"And why should I make arrows for a strange little ragged boy?" grumbled the old man.

However, he made two or three, and

the boy went hunting. In a short time he returned with several small birds. The old woman took them and pulled off the feathers, thanking him and praising him as she did so. She quickly made the little birds into soup, of which the old man ate gladly, and with the soft feathers she stuffed a small pillow.

" You have done well, my grandson! " he said; for they were really very poor.

Not long after, the boy said to his adopted grandmother: " Grandmother, when you see me at the edge of the wood yonder, you must call out: ' A Bear! there goes a Bear! ' "

This she did, and the boy again sent forth one of the magic arrows, which he had taken from the body of his game and kept by him. No sooner had he shot, than he saw the same Bear that he had offered up, lying before him with the arrow in his side!

Now there was great rejoicing in the lodge of the poor old couple. While they were out skinning the Bear and cutting the meat in thin strips to dry, the boy sat alone in the lodge. In the pot on the fire was the Bear's tongue, which he wanted for himself.

All at once a young girl stood in the doorway. She drew her robe modestly before her face as she said in a low voice:

" I come to borrow the mortar of your grandmother! "

The boy gave her the mortar, and also a piece of the tongue which he had cooked, and she went away.

When all of the Bear meat was gone, the boy sent forth a second arrow and killed an Elk, and with the third and fourth he shot the Moose and the Buffalo as before, each time recovering his arrow.

Soon after, he heard that the people of the large village were in trouble. A great

Red Eagle, it was said, flew over the village every day at dawn, and the people

believed that it was a bird of evil omen, for they no longer had any success in hunting. None of their braves had been able to shoot the Eagle, and the chief had offered his only daughter in marriage to the man who should kill it.

When the boy heard this, he went out early the next morning and lay in wait for the Red Eagle. At the touch of his magic arrow, it fell at his feet, and the boy pulled out his arrow and went home without speaking to any one.

But the thankful people followed him to the poor little lodge, and when they had found him, they brought the chief's beautiful daughter to be his wife. Lo, she was the girl who had come to borrow his grandmother's mortar!

Then he went back to the hollow tree where his clothes were hidden, and came back a handsome young man, richly dressed for his wedding.

TWENTY–SEVENTH EVENING
THE GHOST WIFE

TWENTY-SEVENTH EVENING

ON this last evening, the children are told to be especially quiet, and to listen reverently and earnestly, " for these are the greater things of which I am about to tell you," says their old teacher.

" You have heard that the Great Mystery is everywhere. He is in the earth and the water, heat and cold, rocks and trees, sun and sky; and He is also in us. When the spirit departs, that too is a mystery, and therefore we do not speak aloud the name of the dead. There are wonders all about us, and within, but if we are quiet and obedient to the voice of the spirit, sometime we may understand these mysteries! "

It is thus the old sage concludes his lessons, and over all the circle there is a hush of loving reverence.

THE GHOST WIFE

There was once a young man who loved to be alone, and who often stayed away from the camp for days at a time, when it was said that Wolves, Bears and other wild creatures joined him in his rovings.

He was once seen with several Deer about him, petting and handling them; but when the Deer discovered the presence of a stranger, they snorted with fear and quickly vanished. It was supposed that he had learned their language. All the birds answered his call, and even those fairy-like creatures of the air, the butter-flies, would come to him freely and alight upon his body.

One day, as he was lying in the meadow

HE WAS ONCE SEEN WITH SEVERAL DEER ABOUT HIM, PETTING AND HANDLING THEM.

[Page 247

among the wild flowers, completely covered with butterflies of the most brilliant hues, as if it were a gorgeous cloak that he was wearing, there suddenly appeared before him a beautiful young girl.

The youth was startled, for he knew her face. He had seen her often; it was the chief's daughter, the prettiest maiden in the village, who had died ten days before!

The truth was that she had loved this young man in secret, but he had given no thought to her, for he cared only for the wild creatures and had no mind for human ways. Now, as she stood silently before him with downcast eyes, he looked upon her pure face and graceful form, and there awoke in his heart the love that he had never felt before.

"But she is a spirit now!" he said to himself sorrowfully, and dared not speak to her.

However, she smiled archly upon him, in his strange and beautiful garment, for she read his thoughts. Toward sunset, the butterflies flew away, and with them the ghost maiden departed.

After this the young man was absent more than ever, and no one knew that the spirit of the maiden came to him in the deep woods. He built for her a lodge of pine boughs, and there she would come to cook his venison and to mend his moccasins, and sit with him beside his lonely camp-fire.

But at last he was not content with this and begged her to go with him to the village, for his mother and kinsfolk would not allow him to remain always away from them.

" Ah, my spirit wife," he begged, " can you not return with me to my people, so that I may have a home in their sight?"

" It may be so," she replied thoughtfully, " if you will carefully observe my conditions. First, we must pitch our tent a little apart from the rest of the people. Second, you must patiently bear with my absences and the strangeness of my behavior, for I can only visit them and they me in the night time. Third, you must never raise your voice in our teepee, and above all, let me never hear you speak roughly to a child in my presence! "

" All these I will observe faithfully," replied the young husband.

Now it happened that after a longer absence than usual, he was seen to come home with a wife. They pitched their tent some way from the village, and the people saw at a distance the figure of a graceful young woman moving about the solitary white teepee. But whenever any of his relatives approached to congratulate him and to bid her welcome, she would take

up her axe and go forth into the forest as
if to cut wood for her fire, or with her
bucket for water.

At night, however, they came to see
the young couple and found her at home,
but it appeared very strange that she did
not speak to any of them, not even by
signs, though she smiled so graciously
and sweetly that they all loved her.
Her husband explained that the girl was
of another race who have these strange
ways, and by and by the people became
used to them, and even ceased to wonder
why they could never find her at home in
the day time.

So they lived happily together, and in
due time children came to them; first
a boy, and a little girl afterward. But
one night the father came home tired and
hungry from the hunt, and the little one
cried loudly and would not be quieted.
Then for the first time he forgot his

promise and spoke angrily to the mother and child.

Instantly the fire went out and the tent was dark.

When he had kindled the fire again, he saw that he was alone, nor did tears and searchings avail to find his wife and children. Alas, they were gone from him forever!